MEXICO
HUMAN RIGHTS IN
RURAL AREAS
EXCHANGE OF DOCUMENTS
WITH THE MEXICAN GOVERNMENT
ON HUMAN RIGHTS VIOLATIONS
IN OAXACA AND CHIAPAS

Amnesty International Publications

First published 1986 by Amnesty International Publications
1 Easton Street, London WC1X 8DJ, United Kingdom

©Copyright Amnesty International Publications 1986

ISBN 0 86210 098 4
AI Index: AMR 41/07/86
Original Language: English

Printed by Shadowdean Limited, Mitcham, Surrey

The following photographs are copyright: pages 60, 61 © Rafael Doniz; pages 59 (lower), 79 (upper) © Andrés Garay, *La Jornada*; pages 78 (both), 79 (lower), 83 © Oswald Iten, *Neue Zürcher Zeitung;* page 81 © Jesús Morales.

Contents

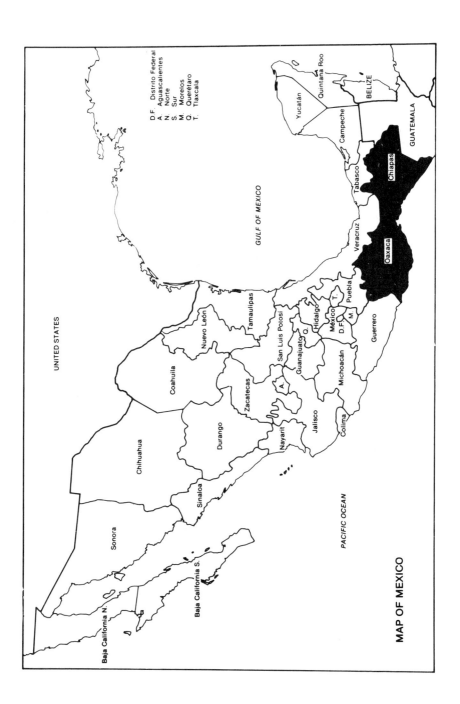

MAP OF MEXICO

D.F. Distrito Federal
A. Aguascalientes
N. Norte
S. Sur
M. Morelos
Q. Querétaro
T. Tlaxcala

UNITED STATES

Baja California N.

Baja California S.

Sonora

Chihuahua

Sinaloa

Durango

Coahuila

Nuevo León

Nayarit

Zacatecas

Tamaulipas

Jalisco

Colima

Michoacán

Guanajuato

San Luis Potosí

Q.

A.

Hidalgo

México

D.F.

M.

T.

Puebla

Guerrero

Veracruz

Oaxaca

Tabasco

Campeche

Yucatán

Quintana Roo

Chiapas

Tlaxcala

BELIZE

GUATEMALA

GULF OF MEXICO

PACIFIC OCEAN

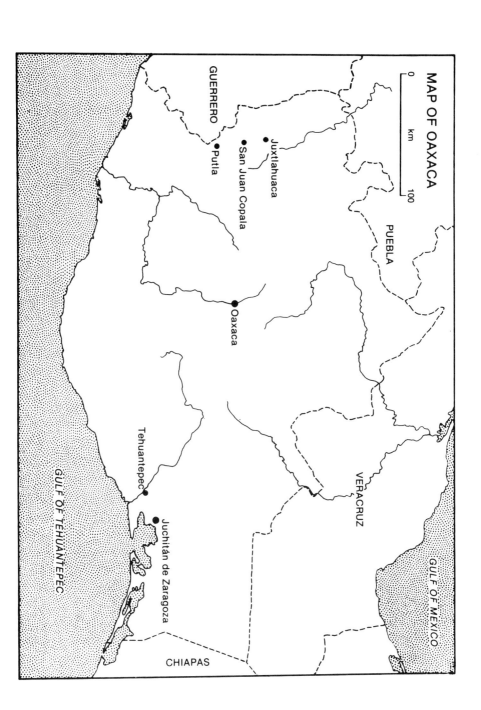

MAP OF OAXACA

0

km

100

GUERRERO

●Putla

●San Juan Copala

●Juxtlahuaca

PUEBLA

●Oaxaca

VERACRUZ

GULF OF MEXICO

Tehuantepec
●

Juchitán de Zaragoza
●

GULF OF TEHUANTEPEC

CHIAPAS

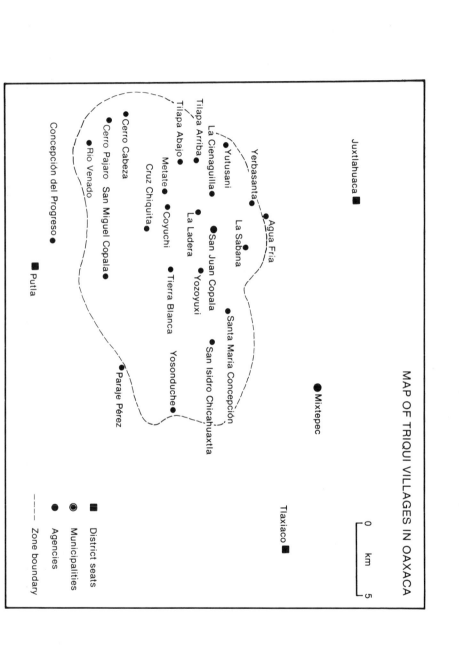

MAP OF TRIQUI VILLAGES IN OAXACA

Juxtlahuaca ■

● Mixtepec

Tlaxiaco ■

Yerbasanta ●
● Agua Fría
La Sabana
La Cienaguilla ●
● Yutusani
● San Juan Copala
Tilapa Arriba
Tilapa Abajo
La Ladera
● Yozoyuxi
Metate ● ● Coyuchi
Cruz Chiquita ●
● Tierra Blanca
● Santa María Concepción
● San Isidro Chicahuaxtla
Yosonduche ●
Cerro Cabeza ●
Cerro Pajaro   San Miguel Copala ●
● Río Venado
Paraje Pérez ●

Concepción del Progreso ●

Putla ■

0 ___ 5
km

■ District seats
◉ Municipalities
● Agencies
----- Zone boundary

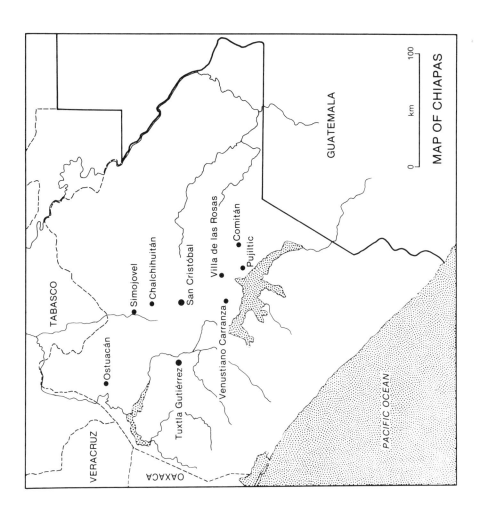

MAP OF CHIAPAS

GUATEMALA

PACIFIC OCEAN

TABASCO

VERACRUZ

OAXACA

Simojovel
Chalchihuitán
San Cristóbal
Villa de las Rosas
Comitán
Pujiltic
Ostuacán
Tuxtla Gutiérrez
Venustiano Carranza

0   km   100

Preface

Over many years Amnesty International has received reports of human rights violations in rural Mexico. Peasants and Indians have reportedly been the victims of political killings and "disappearances", torture, and imprisonment on false criminal charges. Most such reports received recently have come from rural regions in the southern part of the country.

This report comprises the full text of a memorandum submitted on 22 November 1985 to the government of President Miguel de la Madrid Hurtado, and the Mexican Government's reply. The memorandum presents the conclusions of extended research by Amnesty International into human rights violations in the states of Oaxaca and Chiapas in southeastern Mexico.

In March 1984 an Amnesty International research mission visited rural areas in both states to obtain information first-hand. In October of that year the organization sent the President a 45-page document summarizing its concerns in Oaxaca and Chiapas and the findings of the mission. It asked for an opportunity to discuss its concerns directly with government representatives. Replying by telex on behalf of the Mexican Government the then Under-Secretary for Foreign Affairs, Víctor Flores Olea, agreed immediately to Amnesty International's request for a follow-up mission to discuss the document with federal and state government officials. He said, however, that his government found Amnesty International's observations to be inaccurate, distorted and one-sided, and rejected the allegations of human rights violations as unproven and unacceptable.

In January 1985 Amnesty International delegates returned to Mexico and held meetings with senior government officials in Mexico City and in the state capitals of Oaxaca and Chiapas. At the close of the mission, the delegates were given a letter from the Under-Secretary for Foreign Affairs, Alfonso de Rosenzweig-Díaz, replying to Amnesty International's concerns. They were also given detailed legal dossiers on the cases they had raised in both Oaxaca and Chiapas.

The 22 November 1985 memorandum — which is published here

for the first time — addresses the issues discussed during the January 1985 mission, including observations made then by government representatives, and incorporates detailed legal information provided by the Attorney Generals of both states about the cases raised by Amnesty International. It also includes more recent information, including new cases, which appears to substantiate further the pattern of abuses previously observed by the organization.

On 13 January 1986 Amnesty International received a further detailed reply from the Mexican Government in response to its November 1985 memorandum. This consists of two documents providing legal and background information on the new cases raised, as well as further clarification of the cases on which the state governments had already commented during the January 1985 mission. In a covering letter the government reiterated criticisms previously made by Alfonso de Rosenzweig-Díaz following the mission, questioning Amnesty International's objectivity and saying that the organization had displayed an attitude of unwarranted scepticism towards the information provided by the government. At the express request of the Government of Mexico, and in accordance with Amnesty International's established practice of providing governments with the opportunity of a public reply to the organization's concerns, the government's briefing on the states of Oaxaca and Chiapas, and its introductory text, are reproduced as Appendix I of this report.

Amnesty International wishes to place on record its appreciation of the cooperation of the Mexican authorities, both for the facilities placed at the disposal of the members of its delegation which visited Mexico in January 1985, and for the commendable speed and efficiency with which they have responded to Amnesty International's communications. The Secretary General of Amnesty International expressed this appreciation to Alfonso de Rosenzweig-Díaz following the January 1985 mission. Amnesty International attaches great importance to efforts by governments to respond to international bodies promoting respect for basic human rights.

Amnesty International's concerns and the government's response

In its November 1985 memorandum Amnesty International expressed concern at reports of killings and "disappearances" of peasants and members of Indian communities in the states of Oaxaca and Chiapas. The abuses appeared to have occurred as a result of the victims' activities in organizations engaged in land disputes with landowners and local and state authorities. In nearly all cases the killings were carried out by civilians, and not by members of the official security forces. However, Amnesty International was concerned that they had been carried out with the acquiescence of the authorities, to the extent that there had been a consistent failure to detain and prosecute those responsible. Amnesty International was also concerned about frequent reports of the use of torture during police investigations of criminal offences. The organization received information that convictions had been obtained on the basis of confessions extracted under duress while detainees were held incommunicado in police custody. In a number of such cases, after studying the background of the arrest and charges, Amnesty International concluded that the prisoners in question had been detained as a result of their political activities rather than any involvement in the criminal activities imputed to them, and adopted them as prisoners of conscience.

The government replies on cases of political killings and "disappearances" documented in Amnesty International's memorandum give details of criminal investigations opened by local offices of the Public Ministry.[1] In some cases the results are also given of legal proceedings opened against those alleged to be responsible. In the briefing on Chiapas, the authorities also offer a detailed explanation of the background to some of the killings.

Amnesty International accepts that in some of the cases documented in its memorandum, the official information provided indicates that, as far as can be observed, a prompt and thorough investigation was carried out and those directly responsible (or some of them) were brought to justice in accordance with the law. A case in point is that of the massacre of 11 members of an Indian community in Tzacacúm, Chalchihuitán, Chiapas, on 24 March 1983, which is fully documented in the government reply. (See pages 67, 106.) Other killings, notably those which occurred during 1985 in the Comitán region of Chiapas (see pages 69, 115) have also led to the issue of arrest warrants, and some arrests. In many such cases, however, despite the issue of arrest warrants, no efforts appear to have been made to carry out arrests or to proceed with prosecutions. In the Comitán case, for example, warrants had long been issued for the arrest of the alleged killer of peasant leader Andulio Gálvez Velásquez for numerous earlier attacks on peasant leaders, but those warrants had never been enforced.

In general, however, there appears to have been little progress in the investigation of cases of political killings and "disappearances" documented by Amnesty International, particularly

1 The function of the Public Ministry is to investigate and prosecute before the courts crimes under its jurisdiction, request orders of arrest, procure and present evidence against offenders, see that trials are conducted with due regularity and request the imposition of sentence.

4

in the state of Oaxaca. In some of these cases, the authorities, while not denying that the killings occurred, acknowledge that a formal investigation was never carried out, but say that this was due to the failure of the victims or their representatives to register a formal denunciation with the appropriate legal authorities. In the case of killings documented by Amnesty International in the municipality of Villa de las Rosas, Chiapas, they state that the opposition peasant organization of which the victims were members refused to cooperate with the legal authorities and failed to denounce killings to the Public Ministry and to come forward to give evidence. However, the facts available to Amnesty International in a number of such cases do not bear out this assertion.

For example, the authorities deny any legal record of the murder of Elpidio Vásquez on 9 September 1979 in Villa de las Rosas (pages 66, 105). They expressly say that no investigation was carried out because of the lack of a formal denunciation before the proper authorities. However, official documents in Amnesty International's possession indicate that an initial investigation (No.18/979), was opened by the Public Ministry immediately after the killing, and that in a letter dated 11 September 1979 two Agents of the Public Ministry requested an official of the Civil Registry (*Registro de Estado Civil*) to issue a death certificate, describing both the cause of death (craneoencephalic trauma produced by firearm projectile — brain injuries caused by bullet wound) and personal particulars of the victim. (The letter is reproduced on page 77). Amnesty International also has a copy of a statement jointly signed by an official of the municipal police certifying their intention to supervise the burial of the body, of which they had taken charge, in the temporary absence of a higher authority in the town. The statement was copied at the time to the state Attorney General's office.

A further anomaly is apparent in the case of the killing on 29 June 1980 of Alfredo Morales Molina. The investigation of this killing, according to the Chiapas authorities, was filed away on 4 July 1980, only five days after the murder.

In other cases, particularly in the San Juan Copala region of Oaxaca, documents in Amnesty International's possession establish that denunciations and appeals for investigations had in fact been addressed to higher governmental authorities at or near the time of the incidents. (Copies of these documents were sent to the state Attorney General following Amnesty International's mission in January 1985.) Examples of such cases are the reported killing of Marco Ramírez López and the "disappearance" of Juan Martínez López (pages 39, 94). The authorities state that no legal record of these incidents exists. While Amnesty International appreciates the

5

assurances given by the state authorities that further attempts have been made to pursue these cases, it is disappointed that the authorities flatly state that no results were obtained, without giving any information on the steps taken.

In commenting on these cases the state authorities say that written denunciations to federal government authorities (such as the Federal Attorney General or the Minister of the Interior) are not appropriate procedures for the initiation of any preliminary investigation, and that these authorities are not competent to deal with the matter in question. They indicate that for this reason no formal inquiry was undertaken into the alleged crimes. However, while Amnesty International understands that formal criminal investigations in Mexico must be undertaken by the Public Ministry, the federal penal procedural code provides that public officials are obliged, on receiving information that a crime may have been committed, to inform immediately the legal authority empowered to conduct a criminal investigation.[2] It is apparently common in Mexico for members of rural communities to make complaints by sending signed documents to higher governmental officials, including federal officials. In the cases cited, it would appear that such denunciations were not acted on. Furthermore, there is no indication that the officials to which they were addressed forwarded them to the relevant legal authorities.

Deficiencies in official investigations are even more apparent in some cases in which detailed formal denunciations were duly made to the legally constituted authorities. In its letter to the state Attorney General of Oaxaca in March 1985, Amnesty International raised the case again of the "disappearance" of Víctor Pineda Henestrosa (page 52). It provided the authorities with copies of the relevant denunciations giving the name of the Agent of the Public Ministry who had received them and the document number of the initial inquiry. Despite this clarification, the subsequent official reply on the case does not provide any reason to believe that this documentation had been taken into account, or that a serious investigation was carried out (page 103).

Amnesty International believes that torture, although prohibited by the Mexican Constitution and officially condemned, remains in common use by the police forces, particularly as a method to obtain confessions as a basis for criminal prosecutions. Amnesty International expressed particular concern in its memorandum that guarantees against torture, in particular, the authorities' obligation to

2 According to Article 117 of the Federal Code of Penal Procedures, "any person who in the exercise of public functions has knowledge of the probable existence of a crime which must be investigated *ex officio,* is obliged to inform the Public Ministry immediately, and to transmit to it all of the information he or she may have. . .".

6

promptly investigate allegations of torture and bring to justice those responsible, were in practice ineffective.

In many cases, the authorities dismiss allegations of torture documented in the memorandum by indicating that no formal complaint was made by the alleged victim to the appropriate authorities. The government reply confirms that in none of these cases was an investigation conducted by officials on the basis of allegations made through other channels (such as in interviews with journalists, direct appeals by individual petition, delegations, and in writing to government authorities). For example, the alleged torture of Domingo González Domínguez was reported in the press and denounced by members of his organization to the state Governor (pages 43, 98), but no inquiry was carried out. In the case of Gustavo Zárate Vargas (pages 72, 117) the government reply makes no comment on the allegations made by the prisoner, although in this case they were made directly to the judge hearing his case.

In view of its commitments under Article 12 of the United Nations Convention against Torture and Other Cruel, Inhuman or Degrading Treatment or Punishment, Amnesty International believes the Government of Mexico should review the existing procedures for examining and investigating complaints of torture or ill-treatment, so that it can ensure that all such complaints are fully investigated and those responsible brought to justice. In this respect, Amnesty International notes that action *was* taken to investigate charges of torture in the case of Paulino Martínez Delia and that this led to the prosecution of the police officers allegedly responsible (pages 44, 98).

The prevention of torture: recent developments

During 1985 Amnesty International continued to receive reports of torture, the most serious and consistent allegations being made against the Federal District Judicial Police in Mexico City. In September, a number of dead bodies reportedly showing signs of torture were discovered in the ruins of the Federal District Attorney General's headquarters following the 19 September 1985 earthquake which caused extensive damage and loss of life in the capital. The discovery caused a public sensation and led to a renewed media focus on the issue of torture. Draft legislation outlawing torture was submitted to the Senate in November and was passed by this body the following month. At the time of writing it was due to be debated in the Chamber of Deputies, the lower house of Mexico's legislature. Amnesty International was also pleased to learn that on 23 January 1986 Mexico became the second country in the world to ratify the United Nations Convention Against Torture.

In July 1985, Amnesty International wrote to the then Deputy Attorney General of the Republic, Fernando Baeza Meléndez, who was one of the legal officials with whom its delegates discussed the issue of torture during the January 1985 mission. The letter was prompted by grave allegations of torture by Federal District Judicial Police officers which were widely reported in the Mexican press. Cuauhtemoc Estañol Razo, Ignacio del Angel Castellanos and Eduardo Roque Rosario, who were arrested on charges of car theft on 15 April 1985, formally accused three high-ranking police officers of torturing them. They stated that they had been repeatedly beaten, that electric shocks had been applied to sensitive parts of their bodies and that they had been burned with cigarettes while being held for five days in an unrecognized place of detention after their arrest, which was carried out without a warrant. It was further reported that the police and officials of the Federal District Attorney General's office had obstructed them from exercising basic safeguards, such as the right of access to a lawyer, and *amparo* (similar to *habeas corpus*) and that a medical certificate issued by forensic doctors attached to the police department concealed evidence of torture which had been described in detail in a court-appointed doctor's report.[3] Citing other recent cases of a similar nature, Amnesty International concluded its letter by urging that the government adopt special legislation outlawing torture and ensure that it was strictly enforced.

As noted, further evidence of torture came to light when rescue workers discovered a number of bodies while excavating the ruins of the headquarters of the Federal District Attorney General which collapsed during an earthquake which devastated Mexico City on 19 September 1985. One of the alleged torture victims, 19-year-old Johnny Hernández Valencia, was one of a group of Colombians detained on suspicion of belonging to a criminal gang involved in a series of bank robberies and other offences. His mother, Miriam Giraldo Valencia, who had also been detained, told the judge during her first court appearance that they had been tortured by the Federal District Judicial Police while being held incommunicado in a gymnasium in the Attorney General's headquarters. She alleged that the torture had consisted of electric shocks and beatings, and that none of them had been given anything to eat for five days.

Other bodies said to have been found in the ruins with marks of

---

3 In a press interview one of the police officials accused, Lt Colonel David Romero López, denied that the prisoners had been tortured, but openly admitted that torture was routinely used in such cases in order to speed up police investigations. He was quoted as saying: "When we want to torture someone, we give them electric shocks on the tongue or on the testicles, or we burn their piles. But we always take care not to leave marks on the body of the detainee".

torture included that of Ismael Jiménez Pérez, a student of accountancy at the *Universidad Nacional Autónoma de México* (UNAM), National Autonomous University of Mexico, and a lawyer, Saúl Ocampo Abarca, whose body was reported to have been found bound and gagged in the trunk of a vehicle parked in the building's car lot. Following expressions of concern by the Government of Colombia, the Minister of Foreign Affairs, Bernardo Sepúlveda Amor, promised a full inquiry into the allegations of torture of the Colombians. Opposition parties in the Chamber of Deputies called without success for the Federal District Attorney General, Victoria Adato Ibarra, to appear before the legislature to answer questions. In a later public statement, she admitted that there had been no warrant for the arrest of the Colombians, but the Federal District Attorney General's office continued to deny that the detainees had been tortured, citing new forensic evidence which contradicted the finding of an earlier doctor's report. The investigation, the record of which was not made public, was closed in November 1985. No police officers appear to have been charged in connection with the case, but six police commanders, including the officer said to have been responsible for the arrest of the Colombians, were later removed from their posts.

On 19 November a bill outlawing torture was presented in the Senate by the Senate Human Rights Commission. In a press conference members of the Commission affirmed that torture was practised in Mexico. In the following weeks several government representatives, including the Attorney General of the Republic, Sergio García Ramírez, publicly admitted that cases of torture occurred. To Amnesty International's knowledge that was the first time that such an admission had been made by a high-ranking government official. The Attorney General, speaking to journalists, stated that the practice was not institutionalized, in that those responsible were not acting in the name of the federal government, but on their own account, and as such must bear the consequences. He emphasized that his government "has repudiated, repudiates, and will always repudiate any form of human rights violation", and was in full accord with the aims and spirit of the proposed legislation against torture.

The bill proposed by the Senate Human Rights Commission, entitled *Ley Federal para Prevenir y Sancionar la Tortura*, Federal Law for the Prevention and Punishment of Torture, was approved by the Senate in December 1985. Its seven articles include a legal definition of torture, the prescription of a penalty of up to eight years' imprisonment for the offence together with a fine and permanent suspension from duties, recognition of the right of detainees to a medical examination by a doctor of their choice, and a provision that no declaration obtained as a result of torture may be used as evidence in legal proceedings. Article 3 expressly states that no special circumstances or public emergency of any kind can be invoked in justification of torture.

Amnesty International welcomes this initiative which it believes provides a valuable legal reaffirmation of the criminality of torture. Although the practice of torture is formally proscribed in the Constitution, it is not at present expressly envisaged or defined *per se* in the existing penal codes.

While Amnesty International strongly supports legislation against torture, its ultimate value depends on the adoption of measures to ensure that it is capable of being strictly enforced. Since torture most frequently occurs while detainees are held incommunicado in police custody, complaints of torture are often difficult to prove. There is evidence, furthermore, that these practices are often tacitly condoned by officials of the Public Ministry, and the possibility of an impartial inquiry into torture allegations may be prejudiced by the fact that, under the proposed legislation, the Public Ministry would remain responsible for such investigations.

During the Senate debate on torture a series of constitutional amendments were proposed by Senator Manuel Villafuerte Mijangos with the stated aim of eliminating the possibility of torture. A proposed amendment to Articles 16 and 19 of the Constitution would establish specific sanctions against illegal detention, and amendments to Articles 16, 19, 20, 21 and 102 would provide that only the judge be empowered to receive a declaration from a detainee, which must be made in public and in the presence of a defence lawyer, and that statements made to the police during interrogation, or to the Public Ministry would not be admissable as evidence in court. Both the proposed torture legislation and these suggested constitutional amendments have received the support of the Mexican Bar Association.

In October 1983, as part of its Campaign for the Abolition of Torture, Amnesty International adopted a 12-point Program for the Prevention of Torture, which is reproduced in full in Appendix II. The organization has called on governments to implement the program as a positive indication of their commitment to abolish torture and to work for its abolition worldwide. Amnesty International believes the measures contemplated in its 12-point Program to be particularly relevant at a time when the issue of torture and its eradication are a matter of public debate in Mexico. The organization commends the Mexican Government's recent legislative initiatives on torture and hopes that its determination to eliminate this abuse will be made evident by its swift implementation of the measures advocated by Amnesty International.

Human rights in southeastern Mexico:
Conclusions of an Amnesty International investigation into human rights violations in the states of Oaxaca and Chiapas

Introduction

Peasants and Indians in rural Mexico have allegedly been the victims of political killings, torture, unacknowledged arrest and prosecution on false charges, according to reports received by Amnesty International over several years. Most of these alleged abuses took place in states with a large indigenous Indian population where there have been long-standing land disputes. In March 1984 the organization sent a mission to the southern states of Oaxaca and Chiapas to investigate these allegations. The Amnesty International delegates visited Mexico City, the state capitals of Oaxaca and Chiapas, and a number of villages and communities in outlying rural districts. In Oaxaca, the mission concentrated its research on the Triqui Indian community which lives in the isolated rural settlements of San Juan Copala in the municipality of Juxtlahuaca and Putla in the western part of the state. It also visited the town of Juchitán de Zaragoza in the Isthmus of Tehuantepec. In Chiapas, the delegates visited the Simojovel region in the north of the state, and the towns of Venustiano Carranza and Villa de las Rosas in the Central Highlands region (Los Altos). During the mission, the delegates interviewed academics specializing in rural affairs, lawyers, members of the Church and representatives of rural trade unions, peasant organizations and opposition political parties. They spoke to peasants, members of indigenous communities and rural prisoners and their families. Meetings were also arranged with specialists in agrarian affairs attached to federal and state government agencies.

On 31 October 1984 Amnesty International addressed a 45-page memorandum to President Miguel de la Madrid Hurtado summarizing the findings of its mission. The memorandum expressed concern about reports that members of opposition peasant organizations and groups involved in land disputes had been killed in circumstances indicating that they had been extrajudicially executed (deliberately and illegally killed as a result of their political opinions or activities on the orders of, or with the consent of, government authorities). Although some of these killings were alleged to have occurred in incidents involving the police, the majority were apparently carried out by civilians acting with the alleged acquiescence or backing of local authorities. The memorandum also referred to reported instances of unacknowledged arrest and torture in both states. It took up in detail the cases of eight prisoners, all of whom had been charged with or convicted of criminal offences, but who Amnesty International believed to be prisoners of conscience. In a covering letter to the President, Amnesty International asked for the opportunity to return to Mexico to discuss the findings of the memorandum with representatives of the federal and state governments. In December 1984 a reply was received from a senior official of the Ministry of Foreign Affairs which criticized the content and questioned the objectivity of the Amnesty International memorandum, but agreed to the request for meetings with government officials to discuss it in detail.

On 25 January 1985 an Amnesty International delegation headed by the Deputy Secretary General, with Señor Antonio Carretero Pérez, a Spanish judge attached to the Madrid Appeals Court, and two staff members of the organization's International Secretariat, travelled to Mexico. On 28 January they held meetings in Mexico City with senior government officials of the Ministry of Foreign Affairs, the Ministry of the Interior and the Federal Attorney General's office. The following day the delegation, accompanied by federal government officials, travelled to the city of Oaxaca and held meetings with the state Governor of Oaxaca, Lic. Pedro Vásquez Colmenares, and the state Attorney General, Lic. Justiniano Carballido. On the invitation of the Attorney General, the delegates travelled on 30 January to the town of Juxtlahuaca in the Triqui region. There they were given the opportunity to study case dossiers in the office of the Agent of the Public Ministry.[1] On 31 January the delegation arrived in Tuxtla Gutiérrez, capital city of the state of Chiapas, where meetings were held with the state Governor, General Absalón Castellanos Domínguez, and the state Attorney General, Lic. Gustavo Cervantes Rosales.

During the meetings with the Attorney Generals of Oaxaca and Chiapas legal details were made available on almost all of the many

---

1 The Agent of the Public Ministry is a local judicial official responsible to the state Attorney General's office. In accordance with the federal nature of Mexico's Constitution, the state Attorney General's office has jurisdiction over offences under the state penal code, while the prosecution of federal offences is conducted by the Attorney General of the Republic. The function of the Public Ministry, as defined by Article 102 of the Constitution, is to investigate and prosecute before the courts crimes under its jurisdiction, request orders of arrest, procure and present evidence against offenders, see that trials are conducted with due regularity and request the imposition of sentence.

cases documented in the October 1984 memorandum. These included
the results of police investigations into killings and trial proceedings
in cases against rural prisoners. State government officials responded
fully to the delegates' questions regarding trial proceedings, legal
guarantees and remedies and mechanisms for the investigation of
complaints against the police.

On 1 February the Deputy Secretary General of Amnesty International and Señor Carretero returned to Mexico City where they had a
further meeting with officials of the Ministries of Foreign Affairs
and of the Interior. The delegates were given documents summarizing
the material which had been made available by the state Attorney
Generals, and a letter addressed to the Secretary General of Amnesty
International. This reiterated the criticism of the content and method-
ology of the memorandum submitted in October 1984 and criticized
the conduct of the mission. The other two delegates remained in
Mexico for a further week in order to meet non-governmental sources
and to investigate cases of concern to the organization.

This report is based on information received as a result of the
January 1985 mission, and on other information received by Amnesty
International on human rights violations in Oaxaca and Chiapas.
Chapter I summarizes Amnesty International's conclusions regarding political killings, torture, the fairness of trials and political
imprisonment in both states. It includes a number of recommendations which Amnesty International believes could help make human
rights guarantees more effective in rural Mexico. Chapters II and
III deal with specific cases in both states and include legal information provided by the state Attorney Generals of Oaxaca and Chiapas.
These cases are illustrative of the general concerns outlined in Chapter I.

Amnesty International would like to record its appreciation of the
prompt response of the Mexican authorities to its October 1984
memorandum. Its mission in January 1985 received full cooperation
and assistance from the Federal Government of Mexico and the state
governments of Oaxaca and Chiapas. Amnesty International appreciates the repeated assurances given to its delegates of the Mexican
Government's commitment to the protection of human rights. It is
Amnesty International's hope that this avowed commitment will lead
to a serious consideration of the concerns expressed in this report
and to the implementation of its recommendations.

CHAPTER I

Human rights violations
in rural Mexico

In the central and southern states of Mexico, which have a relatively large indigenous Indian population and a standard of living which is well below the national average, a number of peasants and Indians have apparently been the victims of deliberate political killings. Conflicts over land, many of which have persisted for years, form the background to many of these reported killings. Local political disputes within communities have also resulted in violence.

Amnesty International is concerned that some of these disputes have apparently led to deliberate killings of members of peasant organizations in circumstances suggesting that local government authorities were involved. Many of the victims were active in groups pursuing objectives strongly opposed by local landowners and by the local and state government authorities. Most of the killings described in this report were carried out by armed civilians — alleged by representatives of the victims' organizations to be acting in collusion with local landowners and the municipal authorities.

Amnesty International has no evidence that the state government authorities and official security forces participated in the killings. However, it is concerned about consistent reports indicating the involvement of municipal authorities in some of these killings, and about the failure of law enforcement agencies to carry out prompt and effective investigations into killings of members of opposition organizations. As a result, in the majority of these cases, those responsible have never been brought to justice.

Amnesty International has also been concerned about allegations of torture and ill-treatment. Torture is clearly prohibited by the Mexican Constitution. Despite this, reports have reached Amnesty International of detainees being tortured and ill-treated under police interrogation before being presented to a judge for commitment to trial. The methods alleged included beatings and electric shocks, and the purpose was reportedly to obtain "confessions". Amnesty International welcomed several judicial and penal reforms introduced during 1984 to prevent the use of torture. However, it was disturbed by the fact that credible allegations of torture — in some cases presented in complaints to the judge responsible for a case — were not investigated.

In a number of cases constitutional provisions limiting the length of permissible detention before presentation to a judge have been breached. Some arrests were apparently made without a legal warrant, and without informing relatives. Many detainees were reportedly held incommunicado for several days during police interrogation. Amnesty International considers that such practices facilitate human rights violations such as torture.

The Mexican Government has often denied that there are any political prisoners in the country, and that all prisoners are held because of criminal offences. However, Amnesty International has investigated a number of cases in recent years in which it has concluded that criminal charges were brought unjustifiably, and that the real reason for the prisoner's conviction lay in his or her political activities. Amnesty International has therefore adopted a number of prisoners of conscience in rural Mexico, and continues to call for their immediate and unconditional release.

Political killings

In many of the regions where political killings of peasants and Indians have been reported there have been acute and unresolved land conflicts involving Indian communities, *ejidos* (communal land-holdings established as a result of agrarian reform measures) and private landowners. Many of these disputes have persisted for years and have led to sporadic outbreaks of violence. They have often arisen out of the demands for land of landless or semi-landless peasants and have sometimes led to peasants occupying disputed land in the possession of private interests. Violent incidents have also resulted from arguments over land boundaries between neighbouring Indian communities and villages, and from competing and unresolved legal claims to the same tracts of land. In some districts local political disputes between rival factions in the same town or community have broken out after elections for municipal or *ejidal* authorities, and have led to violence.

Amnesty International takes no position on land disputes or on the political issues which have led to such local divisions. However, it is concerned that in some cases such disputes have apparently led to deliberate killings of members of peasant organizations in circumstances suggesting that municipal authorities or members of the security forces were involved. Such killings have not, however, occurred on a massive scale. Although there have been isolated incidents in which large numbers of peasants have been killed, these deaths appear to have been the result of clashes between peasants and security forces during land evictions and similar encounters. Such incidents have been relatively rare in recent years and it is not suggested that such killings have been officially endorsed, or that there is an established pattern of extrajudicial executions of government opponents. Nevertheless, the cases documented in this report suggest that in certain areas, peasants belonging to opposition political groups have been deliberately killed over a period of several years and that in some of these incidents the municipal authorities have been implicated directly or indirectly.

The central and southern states of Mexico have seen a significant growth in recent years in support for peasant organizations established in opposition to the official peasant organization, the *Confederación Nacional Campesina* (CNC), National Peasant Confederation. The CNC is the peasant wing of the *Partido Revolucionario Institucional* (PRI), Institutional Revolutionary Party, which has governed Mexico at the federal and state levels without interruption since 1929 and has rarely lost municipal elections. The CNC has also supplied the great majority of successful candidates for local elected posts, such as the *comisariados ejidales* and *comisariados de bienes comunales*, committees which administer the affairs, property and equipment of *ejidos* and Indian rural communities. In recent years, however, opposition peasant organizations, both affiliated to opposition political parties and independent, have opposed PRI and CNC candidates in local elections. They have also represented villages and communities in land negotiations with federal and state government officials, often in competition with the PRI or the CNC, and have undertaken other political actions, such as demonstrations, marches and public petitions. Most of the victims of killings investigated by Amnesty International were members or supporters of such peasant organizations whose attempts to organize peasant communities independently of official organizations met local opposition.

Many of the victims in the states of Oaxaca and Chiapas were leaders or members of local Indian and peasant organizations associated nationally in the *Coordinadora Nacional Plan de Ayala* (CNPA), the National Plan de Ayala Coordinating body. This was formed in October 1979 to provide an alternative to the official peasant organization and the smaller peasant organizations affiliated to it.

Among the organizations associated with the CNPA whose members have been killed are: the *Movimiento de Unificación y Lucha Triqui* (MULT), Movement for Triqui Unity and Struggle, which is based in the Triqui region of western Oaxaca; the *Coalición Obrero Campesina Estudiantil del Istmo* (COCEI), Worker-Peasant-Student Coalition of the Isthmus, which draws its support from the predominantly Zapotec inhabitants of the Isthmus of Tehuantepec region of Oaxaca; and the *Organización Campesina Emiliano Zapata* (OCEZ), the Emiliano Zapata Peasant Organization, which has been active in various regions of Chiapas. These organizations have campaigned locally and nationally for the implementation of what they claim are presidential decrees establishing titles for communal village lands, which have allegedly been appropriated as a result of illegal transactions by private and commercial interests. They have also campaigned for the expropriation and redistribution of land allegedly acquired illegally by private owners, and for the democratization of community affairs. Another organization whose members have been killed, particularly in Chiapas, is the *Central Independiente de Obreros Agrícolas y Campesinas* (CIOAC), the Independent Union of Agricultural Workers and Peasants. This was formed in 1975 and is affiliated to the largest left-wing opposition party, the *Partido Socialista Unificado de México* (PSUM), Unified Socialist Party of Mexico. The CIOAC has sought to organize landless rural workers, and has campaigned in Chiapas for land and improved wages and working conditions for tied agricultural labourers.

Reports that leaders and members of these organizations have been deliberately killed have been received by Amnesty International for a number of years. Representatives of the MULT list 37 Triqui Indian members of their community assassinated between 1976 and 1981; in Juchitán de Zaragoza in the Isthmus of Tehuantepec in southeastern Oaxaca, 22 members or supporters of the COCEI are said to have been killed in separate incidents between 1974 and 1984; in the Central Highlands region of Chiapas more than 20 Tzotzil peasant leaders have been reported killed since the mid-1960s in the municipal districts of Venustiano Carranza and Villa de las Rosas, according to leaders of the OCEZ and CIOAC, both of which have a considerable peasant following in this region.

An objective of the Amnesty International research mission in March 1984 was to investigate allegations of killings in these regions of Oaxaca and Chiapas, to collect information about the circumstances in which they occurred and to assess the level of official responsibility, if any, for the killings.

In each region a pattern emerged. This indicated that many victims had been killed because of their support for groups pursuing aims opposed by the CNC, by local landowners and commercial interests or by the municipal or state authorities. Some of those killed were known to have been detained previously or wanted for arrest for alleged offences arising out of their political activities. Conflicts had evidently existed for years — sometimes decades — between opposition groups and the municipal or state governments. These conflicts had led not only to the arrest and imprisonment of members of opposition groups, but also to repeated interventions by the army. In some instances, particularly in the state of Oaxaca, troops had allegedly been responsible in previous years for killing members of opposition groups and for "disappearances".

Most of the cases of concern to Amnesty International which are documented in detail in Chapters II and III of this report occurred between 1975 and 1985. The organization has received reports of numerous other killings during this period but has insufficient information to confirm or document them. However, in the majority of cases on which information is available, civilians rather than members of the security forces appear to have been directly responsible for the killings. In the Triqui region of San Juan Copala, Oaxaca, for example, armed civilians — many of whom have been identified by name in documents in Amnesty International's possession as having participated in repeated killings — appear to have been responsible for almost all the killings reported in 1983 and 1984. The armed civilians — often referred to as *pistoleros*[1] (gunmen) — were widely believed to be in the pay of local landowners or "rural bosses".[2] They often allegedly had protection and encouragement from the municipal authorities. Some were said to have held positions in the municipal government, or to be serving auxiliaries of the municipal police. Others appeared to have no official status, but to have violent or criminal backgrounds or to be disaffected members of the community. In some cases, these gunmen allegedly went into action alongside members of the state or municipal preventive police forces. Some habitually used weapons of the type issued to police and soldiers, and allegedly wore police or military-style uniforms. Similar reports of political killings by armed civilians were received from the Central Highland region of Chiapas and from Juchitán, where local PRI members allegedly launched unprovoked armed assaults on COCEI members.

In each area visited by the March 1984 Amnesty International mission, leaders of peasant organizations told them that denunciations of killings rarely, if ever, led to the arrest or prosecution of those

1 In Mexico, the term *pistoleros*, gunmen, is commonly used to denote people who habitually and illegally carry weapons for aggression and physical intimidation, and act on the orders, or under the influence of, private parties.

2 "Rural bosses" is an approximate translation of the Mexican word *caciques*. Frequently themselves landowners, local merchants or self-made peasant leaders, *caciques* are said by many commentators to exert a virtual monopoly of economic and political power at the local level, particularly in remote and inaccessible regions. Although not necessarily holding any official position, many have held elected positions in the municipal government, or are said unofficially to control the election of municipal and village authorities. Experts disagree, however, about the extent of the phenomenon, and the subject remains controversial.

responsible, and expressed considerable scepticism about the possibility of obtaining justice. Many made it clear that they belicved that the gunmen had acted with impunity from the law and with the direct support or acquiescence of the municipal authorities, and that the state authorities had likewise failed to intervene effectively against them. This contributed to the widespread belief among opposition peasant groups that there was collusion between municipal government officials, local officials of the Public Ministry and the state government authorities to draw a veil over the abuses. Peasant leaders claimed that the killings were often falsely portrayed as the result of purely internal feuds and divisions within the communities concerned.

The Amnesty International delegation which visited Mexico in January 1985 raised these concerns with representatives of the federal and state governments, who gave their view of the context in which violence had broken out in several of the rural districts discussed. The state Attorney Generals also provided information on individual killings. This included details of the results of official investigations into the killings documented in Amnesty International's October 1984 memorandum. In most cases the information included the dates on which investigations were begun by the Public Ministry and specified whether orders had been issued by the courts for the arrest of suspects, and when such arrests had been made and suspects charged and convicted by the courts.

In his letter to the Secretary General of Amnesty International, presented at the close of the January 1985 mission, the Under-Secretary for Foreign Affairs, Lic. Alfonso de Rosenzweig-Díaz, rejected any suggestion that there had been official complicity in violent crime or any cover-up. He denied that there was any evidence to support such a view. He stressed that the law had been observed and that the incidents had been investigated and the culprits pursued, detained and prosecuted on an even-handed and impartial basis. In meetings with the Amnesty International delegates state government officials said that the killings described by Amnesty International as political murders were common crimes committed for the most part by peasants or Indians. Officials maintained that they occurred in many cases as a result of internal divisions and feuds within *ejidos* or communities. Others, they said, resulted from grievances with neighbouring groups, sometimes caused by unresolved boundary disputes and competing claims for disputed land. In both states, officials spoke of repeated attempts to find solutions to these problems, which were often legally complex and intractable, and to reconcile the parties in conflict. The Amnesty International delegates were assured that the judicial authorities consistently investigated all such crimes impartially and wherever possible brought those responsible to justice.

Most of the killings reported to Amnesty International were carried out by armed civilians. In one case in Chiapas involving the police, in which two peasants had been killed in the *ejidos* Yotolchén and La Pimienta, a judicial investigation was said to have established that the deaths had resulted from a violent clash in which the police had legitimately used arms to defend themselves against aggression from the peasants. Amnesty International subsequently received reports of a further two incidents in Chiapas in which peasants or settlers were killed by police during land evictions. These took place in the municipality of Pijijiapán between 14 and 16 June 1984 and in Colonia La Granja in Tuxtla Gutiérrez on 16 January 1985. In neither case did the deaths appear to have been the result of deliberate political killings.

Amnesty International has analysed the detailed information provided by the Attorney Generals on the killings documented in its October 1984 memorandum and information received on subsequent killings. It has found no evidence to indicate that the official security forces or the state government authorities have themselves resorted to extrajudicial executions.

However, the available evidence suggests that when members of opposition peasant organizations are killed by armed civilians, those responsible have rarely been brought to justice. Numerous formal and public complaints by community and peasant leaders have accused municipal government officials of complicity in such killings. Although it has not been possible to obtain proven evidence of the involvement of local officials,[1] Amnesty International remains concerned about the strikingly poor success rate of investigations carried out by local agencies of the Public Ministry into these killings. Amnesty International has been able to analyse only a sample of cases, which do not of themselves prove partiality in the administration of justice, or malpractice by local law enforcement agencies. However, the failure to obtain a result from the investigations in those cases strongly suggests that the individuals responsible for the killings may have enjoyed effective immunity from legal prosecution. This failure to impose legal penalties as a result of criminal investigations into killings of peasants identified with opposition groups is also consistent with the concern expressed in the October 1984 memorandum about possible collusion at the local level between law enforcement officials and influential individuals.

Many of the killings reported to Amnesty International did in fact

---

1   In only one case, to Amnesty International's knowledge, was a local government official imprisoned and formally charged with murder following a police investigation (the case of Chalchuihuitán described in Chapter III of this report).

appear to have resulted from internal schisms and feuds within peasant communities, in that the perpetrators and the victims belonged to opposing factions within the same village or community. However, it was frequently alleged that internal divisions within communities were fostered and exploited by landowners closely associated with the municipal authorities. Amnesty International found no direct evidence of official complicity in the killings, but it did note clear differences in the success rate of police investigations, according to the political affiliation of the victim. This strongly suggested a degree of partiality in the conduct and follow-up of criminal investigations in such cases. In the cases studied by Amnesty International, killings of peasants supporting official organizations such as the PRI and the CNC were often followed by the arrest, prosecution and conviction of followers of opposition groups after a swift and sometimes peremptory investigation. Investigations into killings of supporters of opposition peasant organizations, on the other hand, commonly yielded no result, or were delayed for years and subsequently placed on file (*reservada*) for lack of progress. Civilians associated with the local organizations of either the PRI or the CNC were often alleged to be responsible for such killings, but were rarely charged or tried.

The information provided by the state Attorney General of Oaxaca on investigations into killings in the San Juan Copala area confirmed that formal complaints had been presented to the Public Ministry following 15 of the 20 killings recorded in Amnesty International's October 1984 memorandum and that in all cases official investigations were opened. A further two cases, not recorded in the Amnesty International list of killings, were documented in the Attorney General's report, making a total of 17 cases. According to Amnesty International's information, the victims in at least 11 of these cases were MULT supporters, but in these cases only two investigations led to arrests. In all, four people were detained from these two investigations. Arrest orders were issued in one more of these cases, but those named were not detained. In the remaining eight of the 11 cases, the investigations failed to lead to arrest or prosecution. (Some of these cases are described in Chapter II; the remainder are summarized in Table 1.)

In one of the two cases in which arrests were made — that of the murder of Triqui leader, Luis Flores García, in August 1976 — the three defendants were sentenced to 30 years' imprisonment for his murder, but the sentences were later revoked by the state High Court, and they were released.

The official information provided indicates, therefore, that only one person is currently in detention in connection with any of these crimes. No one appears to have been arrested and charged in connection with seven killings of MULT members reported to have been committed since the beginning of 1983.

In three of the remaining cases, in which the victims were said to be PRI members or sympathizers, investigations led to arrests and numerous detention orders. The prisoners who were detained and charged in connection with these murders are all members of the MULT. The official information also shows that a further 40 peasants, also believed by Amnesty International to be MULT supporters, are wanted for arrest on murder charges.

Amnesty International also noted that investigations appeared to be conducted much more quickly and effectively when the victims were associated with the PRI or local authorities. They often led to an arrest and the issue of a custody order within months of the death of the victim. Many of the killings of MULT members, on the other hand, remained unsolved years after they were reported. For example, the investigation into the killing of Camilo Martínez Cruz, a MULT member, was completed only on 25 January 1985, 16 months after his death. Even then, no arrest order appears to have been issued, although both the mother of the victim and two independent witnesses named the same seven people as responsible for his abduction before his death. (Details of the case are given in Chapter II.)

Eight killings in Venustiano Carranza and Villa de las Rosas, in Chiapas, were reported to Amnesty International. All the victims were said to be community leaders working for the recognition of claims to disputed communal land holdings, or supporters of opposition peasant organizations. Of the eight documented killings, information provided by the state Attorney General showed that investigations had been opened in seven cases. Four of the investigations were inconclusive and did not lead to any arrest orders being made. In one case, the investigation appeared to have been placed on file after only four days. In two cases, arrest orders were issued by the judge, but were never enforced. In the remaining case — the only one in which the alleged culprits were detained — the three people in question were committed to prison to await trial, but later absolved by the judge and released. There was an appeal against the judge's verdict and the State High Court revoked the verdict of absolution and sentenced them to nine years' imprisonment. However, those convicted were never rearrested, and 11 years after the date of the crime, successfully applied for the case to be closed. The information indicates, therefore, that in none of the cases under investigation which are summarized in Table 2, were legal penalties imposed as a result of criminal investigations.

As previously stated, Amnesty International recognizes that this analysis is based on a sample of cases and does not in itself prove lack of impartiality in the administration of justice or misconduct by local law enforcement agencies. It does, however, lend weight to the view — frequently expressed to the Amnesty International delegates by members of opposition organizations — that those responsible for these killings have enjoyed effective immunity from prosecution as a result of collusion at the local level between law enforcement officials and powerful individuals to inhibit the due process of law when those they consider "troublemakers" or "agitators" have been killed.

While the above analysis does not provide direct evidence of such collusion, Amnesty International has received other reports which suggest that there has been official acquiescence in the illegal activities of armed civilians in the context of land disputes. There have been several well-documented instances of direct cooperation between official security forces and armed peasants in carrying out arrests and in attempted evictions. In their meetings with federal and state officials the Amnesty International delegates were informed that civilian licences to carry arms are strictly controlled. The Federal Law of Control of Arms and Explosives is enforced in all parts of Mexico by the army. The government representatives stressed that in no circumstances would it be legal or acceptable for the police to act with the assistance of, or in association with, armed civilians. Nevertheless, reports of such incidents continued to be received in 1984, particularly from the Simojovel and Los Altos regions of Chiapas. One particular case, on which Amnesty International received several reports, including an eye-witness account, was the violent armed assault on Maclovio Santis Solano, *comisionado de bienes comunales,* commissioner of communal lands, of San Isidro la Cuchilla in Villa de las Rosas and a CIOAC member, on 5 July 1984. A senior state government official had allegedly authorized armed civilians to arrest Maclovio Santis Solano. They fired on his home and a violent clash ensued in which police officers were killed. Following the incident 14 CIOAC supporters were arrested, but as far as Amnesty International is aware, none of the civilians said to have launched the attack were detained or charged.

During the second half of 1984, Amnesty International received reports of further killings or attempted killings of followers of opposition peasant organizations in the state of Chiapas. In most of these cases those allegedly responsible were gunmen associated with the CNC.

In the San Juan Copala region, Amnesty International recorded a further six killings of Triqui peasants during 1984, alleged to have been carried out by armed civilians.

Details of these incidents were received too late for their inclusion in the October 1984 Amnesty International memorandum, and the organization has not, therefore, had access to the result of any official investigations. However, information from unofficial sources suggests that in most of these cases no arrests have yet been made. One notable exception was the prompt response of the judicial authorities of the state of Chiapas to a multiple killing on 6 October 1984 in Venustiano Carranza. Investigations led to the arrest of 13 peasants affiliated to the CNC faction in the community. However, it was reported in August 1985 that all but one of the defendants had been released. This incident is described in Chapter III.

In most of these recent cases, as in the cases documented in Amnesty International's October 1984 memorandum, representatives of the organizations to which the victims belonged accused armed civilians associated with the CNC or the PRI of being responsible for the killings. Amnesty International has no reason to believe that these killings have been endorsed officially by the CNC or the PRI, or that they were carried out as part of government policy. Nevertheless, the organization is concerned that such allegations have commonly failed to lead to effective official action to bring those responsible to justice and that this may indicate a degree of official toleration of or acquiescence in these abuses.

Reports of similar killings have been received by Amnesty International from other states of Mexico in which conditions are akin to those in Oaxaca and Chiapas, with a large indigenous population, unresolved land demands and the presence of independent opposition peasant organizations. During 1984 Amnesty International received reports of the killing and "disappearance" of Indians and members of dissident peasant organizations in the states of Puebla, Veracruz, Hidalgo and San Luis Potosí. The organization has monitored allegations of killings and "disappearances" of supporters of CNPA-affiliated peasant organizations in the Huastecas region for several years: since October 1983, it has documented 12 such killings in the state of Hidalgo allegedly carried out by armed civilians operating in some cases in concert with members of the official security forces, including the army. From Puebla Amnesty International received reports of the killing of at least 12 peasants from the village of Huizitlán de Serdán in separate incidents in April and May 1984. The victims were said to be members of the *Unión Campesina Independiente* (UCI), Independent Peasant Union, also affiliated to the CNPA. In this case, too, members of the official security forces (the state judicial police) were alleged to have participated in some of the killings, the majority of which were reportedly perpetrated by armed members of *Antorcha Campesina*, Peasant Torch, a peasant organization affiliated to the CNC. It should be pointed out that the governmental authorities have not had the opportunity to comment on these cases — which were outside the scope of the 1984 and 1985 missions.

Amnesty International believes that by failing to ensure that an exhaustive and prompt investigation is carried out in all such cases, and that those responsible are brought to justice on an impartial basis, the government must be considered to share responsibility. Furthermore, although unable to provide direct evidence that municipal authorities colluded in the planning and carrying out of these killings, Amnesty International remains concerned about indications of a permissive attitude on the part of the authorities towards the illegal activities of armed civilians, which has apparently led on occasion to open collaboration with members of the official security forces in combined actions against dissident peasant groups.

Amnesty International believes that the state judicial authorities should review the investigations conducted by local agencies of the Public Ministry into the unsolved cases documented in this report. Further action should be taken to investigate fully any evidence of collusion between law enforcement officials and private parties to instigate such abuses or to obstruct subsequent criminal investigations. If such collusion is found to have occurred, those responsible should be brought to justice in accordance with the law. It is Amnesty International's view that the state authorities are responsible for ensuring that all government officials — at whatever level — obey the law and the Constitution and that the federal governmental authorities are ultimately responsible for ensuring that human rights standards are respected in all parts of Mexico.

Torture and ill-treatment

In its October 1984 memorandum Amnesty International expressed concern about reports of the ill-treatment and torture of detainees in both Chiapas and Oaxaca. Detainees were reportedly tortured and ill-treated while under police interrogation in the period immediately following arrest and before formal commitment for trial. As well as press articles and published testimonies, much of the information was based on interviews with prisoners and their families conducted during the March 1984 mission, when the Amnesty International delegates visited prisons in both states. The memorandum included a number of reports that detainees had been blindfolded and subjected to various forms of ill-treatment and torture, including repeated beatings, the application of electricity to sensitive parts of the body, enforced standing for long periods and the forcing of mineral water up the nostrils. In every case torture was alleged to have been used as a means of obtaining a criminal confession from suspects under police interrogation.

In a number of cases constitutional guarantees limiting the length of detention before the accused must be formally remanded in custody were clearly abused. Some arrests had apparently been made without a legal warrant and without the detainee's immediate relatives being informed of his or her arrest and place of detention. Many of those prisoners were held incommunicado for several days while being interrogated. They had, to all intents and purposes, temporarily "disappeared". Amnesty International believed that such cases, although few in number, were not exceptional — it had previously documented a number of such cases from other states of Mexico, including the Federal District, in which prisoners appeared to have been held incommunicado for days or even months before their detention was made known. Such practices violate Mexican constitutional guarantees and international human rights instruments and are considered by Amnesty International greatly to facilitate serious human rights violations, including torture, "disappearance" and extrajudicial execution.

Ill-treatment during arrest or detention is prohibited by Article 19, paragraph 3, of the Mexican Constitution of 1917; Article 22 outlaws torture of any kind. Article 16 requires that a judicial arrest order must be issued before arrest except when an offender has been caught *in flagrante delicto*, or in other well-defined and exceptional circumstances:

"no one shall be molested in his person, family, domicile, papers or possessions except by virtue of a written order of the competent authority stating the legal grounds and justification for the action taken. No order of arrest or detention shall be issued against any person other than by the competent judicial authority and unless same is preceded by a charge, accusation or complaint from a credible party or by other evidence indicating the probable guilt of the accused."

Article 19 limits the length of the period anyone may be detained without formal charge by establishing that

"no detention shall exceed three days without a formal order of commitment, which shall state the offence with which the accused is charged; the substance thereof; the place, time and circumstances of its commission; and the facts brought to light in the preliminary examination. These facts must be sufficient to establish the *corpus delicti* and the probable guilt of the accused."

26

Finally, Article 20, paragraph 2, expressly prohibits the use of incommunicado detention for obtaining a confession. It states that "no detainee may be forced to be a witness against himself; wherefore denial of access or other means tending to this end is strictly prohibited".

In his letter of 31 January 1985 to the Secretary General of Amnesty International, the Under-Secretary for Foreign Affairs, Lic. Alfonso de Rosenzweig-Díaz, said that the "generalized assertion" that torture and cruel, inhuman and degrading treatment were common in Mexico was false. He went on to point out that when uch abuses came to the attention of the authorities, those responsible were immediately punished. Lic. de Rosenzweig-Díaz also referred to a number of recent reforms of the penal procedural codes which were intended to strengthen existing guarantees against police malpractice.

Amnesty International acknowledges that some progress has been made as a result of a number of recent legal reforms, which are summarized below. However, it is concerned about recurring reports of torture in several states, including Oaxaca and Chiapas, and about specific cases (documented in this report) in which authorities failed to investigate credible torture allegations.

Since its inauguration in December 1982 the government of President Miguel de la Madrid Hurtado has conducted a national campaign against corruption and abuses in public administration and in the conduct of the police and penal system, under the slogan *"renovación moral"*, "moral renewal". The extent of abuses by the police and the loss of public confidence in the honesty and effectiveness of the police forces was the subject of extended public debate in the early 1980s.

The *Dirección de Investigaciones para la Prevención de la Delincuencia* (DIPD), Division of Investigations for the Prevention of Delinquency, a federal plainclothes police force under the direction of the *Dirección General de Policía y Tránsito*, General Directorate of Police and Traffic, has been accused of repeated malpractices, including political abductions and torture. In January 1983 the DIPD was formally abolished and its agents transferred to other police forces. Federal government representatives told Amnesty International that measures were under way to reform or abolish other such irregular police agencies (of which there are many) in an effort to modernize law-enforcement agencies and increase their public accountability. Amnesty International had previously expressed concern at the alleged involvement of one such federal agency, the *Dirección Federal de Seguridad* (DFS), Federal Directorate of Security, in political abductions and torture. Although the mission delegates were told that the DFS, which is under the direct control of the Ministry of the Interior, is purely an investigative agency and does not have legal authority to carry out arrests, Amnesty International continued to receive reports of arrests and torture by DFS officers in 1985.

Other initiatives taken by President de la Madrid included a public consultation on the administration of justice and public security in which noted jurists, penologists and members of the public participated. This resulted in the formulation of a number of important reforms which were subsequently embodied as amendments to the Federal Penal Code and Federal Code of Penal Procedure. They have not, as far as Amnesty International is aware, yet been incorporated into state penal codes and codes of penal procedure. Among the reforms, which were brought to the Amnesty International delegates' attention by the Chief Vice Attorney General of the Republic, is an amendment to Article 279 of the Federal Code of Penal Procedure. This provides that the detainee's confession must now be considered critically by the judge in the light of other evidence and is no longer to be treated as the most reliable evidence ("best evidence"). Amnesty International had expressed concern in its October 1984 memorandum that an unquestioning acceptance by the judge of the first confession as legal proof could facilitate the habitual use of illegitimate methods by police in order to obtain convictions. The organization was interested to read in the official comments on this reform that the Supreme Court has established several precedents denying legal validity to confessions obtained as a result of incommunicado detention and alleged ill-treatment. The previous absence of this essential legal safeguard in Mexican jurisprudence had been noted with concern by Amnesty International in its October 1984 memorandum. Amnesty International also noted the reform to Article 9 of the Federal Penal Code, which establishes the important legal principle that any person charged with an offence is to be considered innocent until proved guilty. The official commentary on this reform points out that Mexican jurisprudence now conforms in this respect to Article 14, paragraph 2, of the International Covenant on Civil and Political Rights. Finally, an addition to Article 128 of the Federal Code of Penal Procedure established that from the moment of arrest detainees must be informed of the charges against them and be told of their right to choose a lawyer for their defence. A detainee's right to access to legal counsel during the police investigation is an important safeguard against illegitimate methods of interrogation, and is a principle which Amnesty International has consistently promoted. Taken together, these reforms are a commendable improvement in the legal guarantees against torture and it is to be hoped that they will shortly be made effective in every state in Mexico.

In Amnesty International's view, however, the eradication of torture depends not only on the formal existence of legal guarantees but also on the will of the government to ensure that they are observed in practice. Law enforcement officials must be made fully aware that torture and ill-treatment will not be tolerated and that if they do occur those responsible will be punished according to the law.

Many Mexican states, including Oaxaca and Chiapas, have agreements with the Federal Attorney General's office on joint programs for training judicial police officers and officials of the state Attorney General's office responsible for criminal investigations. Amnesty International believes that such training programs can be effective if they attach a high priority to observing the legal standards for the treatment of detainees and refer to international agreements signed by Mexico.

The delegates were told that in the Federal District and in some other states the Attorney General carries out periodic unannounced inspections of judicial police detention cells to hear complaints from detainees. The *Visitaduría de la Procuraduría*, Attorney General's Inspectorate, also carries out regular checks on local offices of the Public Ministry in order to detect possible abuses. While recognizing the value of such spot checks as a means of monitoring the treatment of detainees in police custody, Amnesty International believes that in themselves they are not sufficient safeguards against torture. Independent and impartial investigations into credible allegations of torture are also necessary. In analysing the information provided by the Attorney Generals of both states the Amnesty International delegates were struck by the fact that no investigations had been conducted into the allegations of torture or ill-treatment documented in its October 1984 memorandum. These were based on numerous complaints made by prisoners and their relatives in statements published in the national press, in petitions to government authorities, and, in two cases, in signed statements to the judge responsible for the case.

Gustavo Zárate Vargas, whose case is summarized in Chapter III of this report, appealed against the order committing him to custody. In his appeal he made a detailed statement to the judge in which he alleged that he had been tortured while being held incommunicado by the state judicial police in the state Attorney General's headquarters in Tuxtla Gutiérrez. The appeal was rejected and the prisoner was subsequently found guilty on several charges and sentenced by the court. The torture allegations were restated in greater detail by Gustavo Zárate Vargas when he was interviewed in prison by an Amnesty International delegate. The Amnesty International delegates examined the judicial transcripts of the case provided by the state Attorney General of Chiapas and pointed out to him that the statements attributed to the accused Gustavo Zárate Vargas, which the prisoner claimed were extracted under torture, appeared indeed scarcely credible as voluntary statements. However, Amnesty International learned from the state Attorney General that no investigation had been carried out into these torture allegations. In commenting on this case, the state Attorney General assured the Amnesty International delegates that an investigation would have been carried out had the defendant made a formal complaint to the Agent of the Public Ministry, but in this case no such complaint had been made. Despite the fact that the court record clearly discloses that a complaint was made to the judge, this was evidently not considered sufficient procedural grounds for an official investigation. The state Attorney General indicated that in the absence of any formal complaints to the Public Ministry there had been no recent investigations or proceedings against police officers accused of torture or ill-treatment. The Attorney General asserted categorically, in fact, that torture did not take place.

The Government of Mexico has cooperated with international efforts to curb the practice of torture. In June 1980 it unilaterally declared its intention to comply with the United Nations Declaration on the Protection of All Persons from Torture and Other Cruel, Inhuman or Degrading Treatment or Punishment, and the following July responded to the United Nations questionnaire on torture by providing information on legal guarantees and measures taken to prevent torture in the Constitution, criminal procedural codes and legislation governing the prison system. It did not, however, provide any information on whether, since the adoption of the Declaration, any investigations had been carried out or proceedings instituted with regard to allegations of torture.

Article 9 of the United Nations Declaration Against Torture specifically sets out the responsibilities of governments to investigate allegations of torture:

"Wherever there is reasonable ground to believe that an act of torture as defined in Article 1 has been committed, the competent authorities of the State concerned shall promptly proceed to an impartial investigation even if there has been no formal complaint."

On 18 March 1985 the Government of Mexico signed the United Nations Convention against Torture and Other Cruel, Inhuman or Degrading Treatment or Punishment, adopted by the General Assembly on 10 December 1984. Under the Vienna Convention on the Law of Treaties (1969), this entails the obligation of the state to refrain from acts which would defeat the object and purpose of a treaty, prior to its entry into force. Article 12 of the United Nations Convention also refers to the obligation of the government authorities to carry out a prompt investigation whenever there are reasonable grounds for believing that torture has taken place.

Both the United Nations Declaration and the Convention Against Torture clearly establish that governments have a responsibility to intervene *actively* to ensure that allegations of torture are promptly and fully investigated. The reasoning behind this prescription is explained in Amnesty International's report *Torture in the Eighties* (1984) which documents evidence of torture around the world and analyses steps towards its eradication:

"If detainees' allegations are largely propaganda, however, then the expenditure of resources to establish the facts and put them before the public would enhance, not sully, the reputation of the security forces. It is self-evident that there is a potentially gross imbalance of power between a detainee and his or her captors; it is likewise obvious that the state has infinitely more investigative resources than an individual detainee. It follows that a government's determination formally to investigate complaints against its security forces and to report publicly on those investigations would go a long way, albeit after an alleged injury had occurred, to correct that imbalance of power and resources.

"Secondly, if some form of official complaints machinery does exist, there may be a reluctance on the part of detainees and former detainees to use it. Victims of torture may fear reprisals from the security forces, and sometimes ill-treatment in custody is not reported because the victim does not believe that it will do any good. They may believe that the word of a security official will be given more weight in court than their own testimony. . . Therefore, complaints procedures should provide for an investigation of allegations where there is reasonable ground to believe that torture has occurred, even if formal complaints have not been lodged." (Page 80)

In view of the legislative improvements introduced by the present government in Mexico, Amnesty International hopes that the authorities will ensure that all credible allegations of torture are promptly, vigorously and impartially investigated, regardless of whether a formal complaint has been made. Amnesty International believes that the results of such investigations, and the methods by which they were obtained, should be widely publicized.

Furthermore, measures should be adopted to ensure that detainees are promptly informed, after arrest, of their right to register complaints in case of ill-treatment and that such complaints can be made without fear of reprisals against the detainee or his or her family. In this respect, the addition to Article 128 of the Federal Code of Penal Procedure, upholding the detainee's right to access to a lawyer during the police investigation, is an important advance. In Amnesty International's view its implementation as routine procedure in every state of Mexico, for common as well as federal offences, would provide an important additional safeguard against ill-treatment and torture.

Political imprisonment and trials

The Mexican Constitution of 1917 provides a framework of legal guarantees protecting civil and political rights. Article 6 states that "the expression of ideas shall not be subject to any judicial or administrative investigation, unless it offends good morals, infringes the rights of others, incites to crime, or disturbs the public order". Article 7 establishes that "the freedom of writing and publishing writings on any subject is inviolable. No law or authority may establish censorship". Articles 8 and 9, respectively, protect the right to petition and the right to assemble or associate peacefully for any lawful purpose. Political rights are further defined in the Act on Political Organizations and Electoral Processes (1977) which extended the participation of opposition parties in the electoral and political process. This law regulates the constitution of political parties and requires them to register.

The articles of the Constitution guaranteeing individual rights have been in force without interruption since the Second World War, when they were temporarily suspended between 1942 and 1945.

Under Article 144 of the Federal Penal Code "political offences" are limited to the crimes of rebellion, sedition, mutiny and conspiracy to commit them, all of which are classified as crimes against the security of the nation, and all of which imply the use of violence. There is no provision in the penal codes or in other legislation limiting or curtailing non-violent forms of political association and expression.

The Mexican authorities have frequently denied that there are any political prisoners in Mexico, maintaining that all prisoners have been detained for, or convicted of, criminal offences under the federal or state penal codes.[1] They state that although the actions which led to a prisoner's conviction may, in some cases, have been politically

---

1   Amnesty International understands the term "political prisoner" to include anyone who is imprisoned where the motivation of the authorities appears to be political or where the acts or the motivation for the acts of the prisoner appear to be political. Amnesty International calls for fair and prompt trials for all political prisoners.

motivated, the imprisonment resulted, not from political views or lawful political activities as such, but from breaking criminal laws. This interpretation is widely contested, however, in Mexico. Human rights groups and opposition parties often argue that members of political organizations and trade unions have been detained and prosecuted for criminal offences on the basis of false evidence, or confessions obtained under duress, and that the real reason for their imprisonment was political.

In recent years Amnesty International has itself investigated numerous cases where there were reasons to believe criminal charges may have been brought unjustifiably against individuals for political reasons. In such cases, Amnesty International examines the political context of the case, the nature of the accusations and the evidence on which these were based and the existence, or otherwise, of irregularities in the trial proceedings.

In its October 1984 memorandum Amnesty International described the cases of seven prisoners detained in the states of Oaxaca and Chiapas which the organization was investigating, and eight other cases of adopted prisoners of conscience.[1] In each of these cases, Amnesty International was concerned about inadequacies and delays in the judicial proceedings followed. During its mission to Mexico in January 1985 detailed legal information was provided by the state Attorney Generals on each of these cases.

Most of these prisoners are Indians and members of dissident peasant organizations who were detained on murder charges after killings of members of their own communities or ethnic groups. In each case, arrest and trial proceedings followed complaints formally registered by alleged witnesses to the killings, whose declarations formed the basis of the charges against the accused. The Amnesty International delegates noted that in all of the communities studied, a large number of dissident peasant or Indian leaders — and members of their organizations — had been repeatedly named in such declarations. Many of these people had detention orders served on them or had previously spent time in prison on various criminal charges. Some of them were separately named and accused in relation to several criminal investigations or trial proceedings.

Amnesty International was concerned about several aspects of the trial proceedings relating to these individuals. In studying the avail-

---

1 "Prisoners of conscience" refers to those prisoners who, in Amnesty International's view, have been imprisoned as a result of their beliefs, colour, sex, ethnic origin, language or religion, who have not used or advocated violence. In Mexico several such prisoners have been imprisoned, Amnesty International believes, because of non-violent political activities, and faced criminal charges which appeared to be unfounded or based on dubious or insufficient evidence. Amnesty International calls for the immediate and unconditional release of all prisoners of conscience.

able case dossiers on five Triqui prisoners who were members of the MULT, it noted that the principal evidence against the accused consisted of statements by alleged eye-witnesses which seemed either implausible or questionable. As in other similar cases, such testimony invariably formed the basis of police investigations into alleged killings and led to a judge issuing arrest warrants after the Agent of the Public Ministry had decided on the "probable guilt of the accused". The Amnesty International delegates were struck by one case against four Triquis accused of a murder on 24 July 1983 in the village of Cruz Chiquita. The case against the defendants appeared to rest on the evidence of four alleged eye-witnesses, each of whom listed 25 people they claimed to have seen ambushing the victim, who they claimed they were accompanying at the time. All 25 were separately named by each witness in the same order. When called to a confrontation with one of the accused, one of the witnesses whose previous testimony had led to the prisoner's arrest was unable to identify or recognize him. Several of the alleged witnesses who had ratified their initial declarations later failed to appear to undergo cross-examination by the defence or attend confrontations with the accused. (This case is described in greater detail in Chapter II.)

It is evident that the reliability of this type of evidence depends to a large extent on the circumstances in which it was obtained and on the opportunities available to the defence to cross-examine the prosecution witnesses. Lawyers consulted by Amnesty International have drawn attention to the potential distortions of both prosecution and defence testimony resulting from the fact that, in many such cases, both parties may be illiterate and speak only an indigenous language, while all the legal proceedings are conducted in Spanish. As a result, the accuracy of interpreters employed by courts and by local offices of the Public Ministry, who transcribe into Spanish statements made in indigenous dialects, is crucial. A further factor, confirmed in discussion with the state Attorney General of Oaxaca, is that many Indian prisoners must rely for their defence on a court-appointed official without legal training, since in many regions qualified lawyers are not available to undertake this work.

Amnesty International recognizes the inherent difficulties in ensuring prompt and impartial criminal investigations when offences are committed in remote and inaccessible villages, and when trial proceedings are further complicated by language barriers and illiteracy. However, it must be recognized that these factors also significantly increase the risk that witnesses may be manipulated, knowingly or unknowingly, by third parties interested in obtaining a conviction for personal or political reasons. It was frequently alleged by representatives of peasant organizations that the authorities had arbitrarily detained their members on trumped-up charges, falsely accusing them of crimes committed in the region. While Amnesty International was not in a position to substantiate such allegations, it noted a pattern involving a significant number of prisoners who were held for long periods on charges which were eventually dismissed by the court. In the case of the Triqui prisoners, for example, Amnesty International found that trial proceedings were not normally completed until well over a year after their arrest. In some cases the delay extended to several years despite the fact that the Mexican Constitution prescribes a maximum period of one year for completion of trial proceedings even for the most serious offences. Prisoners held on unfounded charges in such cases would be subject to an extended period of imprisonment, particularly if they were unable to obtain the services of a defence lawyer to press for a speedy resolution of their case. Four of the five Triqui prisoners whose case Amnesty International began investigating in 1984 were released in 1985 after the judge dismissed the charges against them. All of them had been held for longer than the maximum period of one year prescribed by the Constitution.

Another case in which Amnesty International is concerned about delays in trial proceedings is that of four COCEI members — Jesús Vicente Vásquez, Leopoldo de Gyves Pineda, Carlos Sánchez López and Manuel Vásquez Nicolás — who were arrested in December 1983 and were not brought to trial until August 1985, when the last three prisoners were released unconditionally after being found not guilty. Each had been adopted as a prisoner of conscience. (This case is described in Chapter II.)

Amnesty International welcomed news that two other adopted prisoners of conscience in the state of Chiapas were released shortly after the January 1985 mission. One was Gustavo Zárate Vargas, a 30-year-old economics lecturer at the state university, who was released on 1 March 1985 after a successful *amparo*[3] appeal to the Supreme Court of the Nation which reduced his sentence from seven and a half years to two years three months. The other was José Manuel Hernández Martínez, an OCEZ member and community leader from Venustiano Carranza, who was released on 23 February 1985. He had been accused of the murder of a peasant in June 1980,

---

[3] *Amparo* (roughly translated as *habeas corpus*) is commonly used in Mexico as a legal recourse against laws or official acts which are believed to violate individual guarantees. It is wide in scope, and includes not only legal remedies against illegal arrest and detention, but also the possibility of an appeal against a final court sentence where the court proceedings or the sentence itself are held to violate such guarantees. In the case of federal offences, the *amparo* appeal in such cases is made directly to the Supreme Court of Justice.

but Amnesty International believed he had in fact been arrested as a result of his political activities as a local community leader. Amnesty International had also adopted two other members of his organization — Victórico Hernández Martínez and Agustín de la Torre Hernández — as prisoners of conscience. They were sentenced in November 1983 to 12 years' imprisonment for the same offence. In their case as well, Amnesty International believes that they were prosecuted because of their role as leaders of their community. The organization noted numerous inconsistencies in the evidence against them which consisted of statements by witnesses, all of whom belonged to the opposing political faction in Venustiano Carranza. The appeals court confirmed the sentence against Victórico Hernández and Agustín de la Torre in January 1984. After this decision, both prisoners filed a petition for *amparo* against the sentence to the Supreme Court of the Nation. By June 1985 the Supreme Court had not pronounced its verdict on the petition. The two prisoners are serving their sentence in Cerro Hueco prison in Tuxtla Gutiérrez. Their cases, and those of the other Chiapas prisoners of concern to Amnesty International, are described in Chapter III.

Amnesty International recognizes that special difficulties exist in ensuring prompt and fair trials in rural areas, where many prisoners do not understand the language in which trial proceedings are conducted or the legal concepts on which they are based. It believes, however, that fair trial guarantees could be strengthened in such cases by ensuring that from the moment of arrest detainees are fully informed, in their own language, of the charges against them and of their rights of defence and appeal, by making more qualified legal assistance available to detainees and by ensuring that trials are completed within the constitutionally prescribed period.

CHAPTER II

Evidence of abuses in the state of Oaxaca

This chapter deals with instances of alleged human rights violations in the state of Oaxaca on which Amnesty International has collected detailed information. Most of the cases documented were included in the memorandum submitted by Amnesty International to the Government of Mexico in October 1984, following its research mission to Oaxaca in March of that year. Detailed reference is made to the official information on individual cases made available by the state Attorney General to Amnesty International's delegates during its January 1985 mission. Some additional cases are included on which Amnesty International received information too late for their inclusion in the October 1984 memorandum, and on which representatives of the state government have not, therefore, had the opportunity to comment.

The first section of this chapter is devoted to Amnesty International's concerns in the Triqui region of Western Oaxaca; the second section to its concerns in the Isthmus region in the southeastern part of the state, in particular the town of Juchitán de Zaragoza. Both are regions from which Amnesty International has received persistent reports of human rights violations in recent years.

San Juan Copala

In its October 1984 memorandum Amnesty International drew attention to reports it had received over a number of years of human rights violations inflicted on members of the Triqui indigenous group who live in the hamlets and settlements of San Juan Copala in the municipal districts of Juxtlahuaca and Putla in western Oaxaca. The reported abuses included: killings of peasants in Triqui villages in the course of armed incursions by troops, police and gunmen; premeditated assassinations of Triqui peasant leaders in ambushes; torture, rape and ill-treatment.

Triqui community representatives repeatedly denounced such abuses and, in the period from 1978 to 1982, appealed to the state government authorities of Oaxaca and to the federal authorities to intervene. At this time many of the abuses were allegedly perpetrated by soldiers belonging to army units attached to the 28th Military Zone, who were stationed in San Juan Copala, acting in collaboration with the municipal authorities. The settlements said to be most affected were Cruz Chiquita, Rastrojo, Coyuchi, Agua Fría, La Cienaguilla, Río Tejón, Santa Cruz Tilapa, San Miguel Copala, Río Metate, Llano de Nopal, Yutusani and Yozoyuxi. The abuses reportedly became much more frequent in the months leading up to municipal elections in San Juan Copala, which took place on 26 December 1982 and which were contested unsuccessfully by the *Movimiento de Unificación y Lucha Triqui* (MULT), the Movement for Triqui Unity and Struggle. According to a list published in 1982 by the MULT, 37 Triqui Indians from hamlets in the San Juan Copala area were murdered in separate incidents between July 1976 and December 1981. Most of the reported victims (28 of them) came from three hamlets: Santa Cruz Tilapa, Yozoyuxi and Yutusani. In 1982 reports of a further eight killings were received by Amnesty International.

During 1983 and 1984 reports of abuses allegedly committed by the army declined. Nevertheless, the pattern of reported killings, attempted killings, harassment and torture of Triqui Indians continued. Those alleged to be responsible were civilian gunmen with the apparent support of the municipal authorities, and members of the official security forces, including the municipal and state preventive police. The main victims were said to be Triqui peasant farmers living in isolated settlements, many of whom speak little or no Spanish. Many of them were Triqui community leaders taking a strong stand on political and economic issues, who were asserting claims for what they maintained were their community lands illegally usurped by owners of private estates and local authorities. More recently, leaders and supporters of the MULT have been among the victims. This organization was founded in 1981 and has since campaigned nationally and in local elections in San Juan Copala on the issue of the Triquis' title to 13,705 hectares of disputed woodlands and communal land.

Political killings and torture of Triqui Indians

According to statements published by the MULT most of the recent killings were carried out by armed civilians who have been frequently named in complaints to the authorities. They were alleged to have had the support or acquiescence of the municipal authorities of San Juan Copala. Members of the state or municipal police forces were alleged to have participated in two killings, together with civilians allegedly wearing police uniforms, who were said to have been recognized by local people. Several of them have indeed been repeatedly named by community leaders in appeals to the state authorities.

Some killings are said to have taken place during armed raids on villages, in which peasants were shot at, homes and crops have been burned and villagers harassed and intimidated. Peasants were reportedly shot and killed arbitrarily in order to intimidate or punish them. Other killings are said to have taken place in ambushes along the roads linking the hamlets of San Juan Copala. The victims were apparently selected because of their political beliefs or activities and were reportedly shot and left for dead on the road or in the fields. Other killings were reported after the victims had been abducted by armed civilians alleged to have been acting with the prior knowledge or acquiescence of local government authorities. The circumstances of killings in all these categories were frequently reported to the state authorities by relatives and MULT representatives who maintained that the authorities had failed to investigate them satisfactorily. This alleged failure appeared to contribute to a widespread belief that there was collusion between private interests, the state and municipal governments and the local judicial authorities, and that the culprits had virtually been given legal immunity. MULT representatives categorically rejected the view, which they claimed had been repeatedly expressed by government officials, that the killings were the result of long-standing and violent internal conflicts within the Triqui community, and that the authorities were doing their best to investigate them impartially and bring those responsible to justice.

Amnesty International has also received reports of torture and ill-treatment of Triqui peasants when they were being arrested by police and while they were being held for questioning on criminal charges. Villagers are also reported to have been tortured, raped and ill-treated by armed civilians, sometimes allegedly accompanied by police, because of their political activities or sympathies. In such cases, ill-treatment appears to have been used to intimidate villagers and deter them from joining the MULT, or as a means of extorting money from them. Some of the civilians allegedly responsible for these abuses were also said to have carried out killings in the region, and they were also believed to be associated with the municipal authorities of San Juan Copala.

In March 1984, Amnesty International sent a mission to San Juan Copala, and in its memorandum of 31 October 1984 appended a list of 16 killings reported between April 1983 and March 1984. Summary details were given of nine of these cases, of which two dated from previous years.

During its subsequent mission to Mexico in January 1985 the Amnesty International delegates were given detailed information by the state Attorney General's office on all of these cases. From this information, the organization was able to confirm the deaths in all but a small number of cases, and to ascertain the results, if any, of official investigations conducted by local Agencies of the Public Ministry responsible to the state Attorney General.

Amnesty International is concerned about the evident failure of the authorities to bring those responsible for these killings to justice in most of these cases, and by the apparent reluctance to investigate vigorously allegations of killings made by representatives of opposition peasant groups. In the cases summarized below the authorities appear on occasion to have failed to investigate detailed allegations of killings, and there have been long delays in the conduct of criminal investigations. These have either remained inconclusive, or failed to lead to any arrests. With regard to cases of ill-treatment and torture no firm conclusion could be drawn: many cases appeared not to be reported to the judicial authorities or, when they were reported, failed to lead to any investigation. One case on which Amnesty International reported, that of Paulino Martínez Ramírez and his wife, María Francisca, did, however, result in the arrest of two people who were among those alleged to be responsible.

Cases

Luis Flores García
The number of political murders in San Juan Copala appeared to increase markedly after the assassination on 11 August 1976 of Luis Flores García, a Triqui who had been an elected community leader before his death. The murder took place in the hamlet of Paraje Pérez and was allegedly committed by a group of civilians said to have been hired by local landowners. Luis Flores García had led community efforts to assert claims to what the community maintained were communal lands and had been involved in attempts to set up a marketing cooperative.

Information provided by the state Attorney General indicated that criminal proceedings were instituted against four civilians accused of his murder. One was never arrested; three of those accused were detained and subsequently sentenced to 30 years' imprisonment for assault and murder. They appealed against the sentence and on 26 January 1979 the state High Court quashed the sentence and they were released.

Marcos Ramírez López
Marcos Ramírez López was allegedly murdered on 29 February 1980 in Concepción Carrizal, San Juan Copala. Roberto García López, a peasant, claimed to have been abducted with Marcos Ramírez López and to have witnessed his killing. Roberto García López later signed

a detailed statement to the municipal police of San Miguel Copala. He stated that both he and Marcos Ramírez López, from the village of Río Metate, had left San Juan Copala after detention orders were issued against them and were working as casual labourers in Culiacán, state of Sinaloa, at the time of their abduction.

He claimed that Sinaloa state police officers, accompanied by a group of armed civilians from San Juan Copala who were well known to him, forcibly detained him and Marcos Ramírez in Culiacán, Sinaloa, on 27 February 1980. He maintained that they were both beaten by the civilians, who raped Marcos Ramírez' wife in the presence of the police and robbed her of her wages. The two prisoners were then said to have been taken by police car to a jail, where they were handed over to the civilians, who then took them to the hamlet of Concepción Carrizal, near San Juan Copala. On 29 February at about 3am Marcos Ramírez López was allegedly taken out of the room where they were being held captive and shot. Roberto García stated that he managed, still handcuffed, to escape his captors, who had been drinking heavily.

According to the information provided by the state Attorney General on this case, the victim's mother informed the Agent of the Public Ministry that Marcos Ramírez López had disappeared on 5 June 1983. She said that he had disappeared after leaving for the fields and that she considered it likely that he had fled to escape arrest, since there was a detention order issued against him. In commenting on this case to the Amnesty International delegates, the state Attorney General indicated that he considered the account given above of Marcos Ramírez' arrest in Sinaloa and subsequent murder in Oaxaca highly implausible in view of the improbability of collaboration between civilians and police officers from another state, and of the distance the civilians would have had to travel to take their captives back to San Juan Copala. Amnesty International raised this case again in a letter to the state Attorney General of March 1985, attaching a copy of Roberto García's statement. A copy was also enclosed of a complaint sent by a village leader and a large group of neighbours to Lic. Oscar Flores Sánchez, then Federal Attorney General. This contained a similar account of the circumstances of the alleged killing. Copies of both documents were evidently forwarded at the time to the state judicial authorities. No reply has been received to Amnesty International's letter to the state Attorney General, and the organization has received no indication that the allegations made by Roberto García were properly investigated.

Juan Martínez López

Juan Martínez López, a MULT leader from the village of Yozoyuxi, was reported to have "disappeared" on 8 November 1981 on his return journey from Mexico City, where he had been negotiating on behalf of his organization with officials of the Ministry of the Interior. According to the available reports he was returning to San Juan Copala to collect money for a delegation to go to Oaxaca for talks with state government officials, and "disappeared" after being detained by a group of civilians as he got off a bus close to the hamlet of Concepción Carrizal, near Yozoyuxi. On 2 December 1981 a formal complaint was sent by a lawyer, Lic. Carlos Fernández del Real, to the then Minister of the Interior, Prof. Enrique Olivares Santana, identifying by name four individuals said to be responsible for his abduction and "disappearance". In his letter Lic. Fernández del Real referred to a written complaint regarding the "disappearance" of Juan Martínez López made in November 1981 by Triqui representatives to the state Governor of Oaxaca. He also mentioned an eyewitness, who did not wish to be identified, who claimed to have seen the same four individuals murder Juan Martínez López with their machetes. The state Attorney General of Oaxaca told the Amnesty International delegates in January 1985 that there was no record of the case. Following its mission in January, Amnesty International sent the state Attorney General a copy of Lic. Fernández del Real's letter, asking for information of any inquiry into the fate of Juan Martínez López. No reply has been received from the Attorney General, and again there is no indication of any investigation being conducted.

Camilo Martínez Cruz
Camilo Martínez Cruz, a MULT leader from the village of Santa Cruz Tilapa, was reported to have been detained on 5 September 1983 in San Juan Copala by three individuals claiming to be members of the municipal police. According to a complaint by his mother, María Florencia Cruz, to the state Attorney General on 15 December 1983, she found her son dead in San Juan Copala on 6 September 1983, the day after he was seized. She stated that his body showed marks of torture. In her statement she identified several individuals allegedly responsible for the arrest of her son. Three of them had been cited in accounts of other abuses in the area as close collaborators with the municipal police and local authorities of San Juan Copala. Information provided by the state Attorney General indicated that an investigation into the killing of Camilo Martínez Cruz had been initiated on 9 September 1983. The victim's mother had made a statement accusing eight people of responsibility, and two other witnesses had also made declarations against them. The preliminary investigation was completed and deposited on 25 January 1985. Legal officials in Juxtlahuaca consulted by the Amnesty International delegates were unable to provide details of the results of the investigation, but to Amnesty International's knowledge it has not yet led to any arrest.

42

Paulino Martínez Ramírez and María Francisca
On 21 February 1984 community leaders of Llano de Nopal made a detailed complaint to the Municipal President of Juxtlahuaca. It concerned reported abuses by a group of six individuals who they said had been acting with the support of the municipal authorities of San Juan Copala. On 8 and 28 March 1984 further letters were sent to the state Governor of Oaxaca describing four separate incidents in February and March of that year in which the same individuals, sometimes allegedly in police uniforms and carrying police weapons, had beaten and threatened peasants in order to extort money. On two occasions peasants' wives were said to have been raped in their presence. According to the account given of one such incident:

"On 6 March of the present year at 13.00 hours in the morning, the assailants suddenly arrived at "Llano Grande", the home of Señor Paulino Martínez Ramírez, and his wife, María Francisca. They tied up Señor Martínez and beat him brutally until he was left senseless and beat María Francisca and savagely raped her. After an hour María Francisca thought her husband had died. They dragged him away to the centre of the village and then left him abandoned in the jail. When, a few hours later, Paulino Martínez came round, he was still in jail. They stole all his belongings and money in cash — a total amount of 100,000 pesos. After every sort of punishment, he had to pay another 15,000 pesos to be released."

Official information provided by the state Attorney General shows that a police investigation of this incident led to the issue of arrest orders against two of those named on charges of breaking and entering, robbery, wounding and rape. Amnesty International subsequently received information that two of the others named are currently in detention in Juxtlahuaca and Putla, at least one apparently detained in connection with this incident. It was later reported that María Francisca was murdered in her home on 1 July 1984, apparently in reprisal for her husband's role in denouncing the abuses which led to the arrests. Amnesty International has, however, not been able to confirm reports of her murder, which was not mentioned in the Attorney General's information on the case.

Juan Albino
Juan Albino, reportedly a MULT supporter, is said to have been detained with another peasant, Julio Hernández López, on 9 December 1983, in the village of La Ladera, by police accompanied by armed civilians. Their associates described what happened to them afterwards as follows:

"The people arrested in La Ladera were taken away by two *pistoleros* from San Juan Copala. They tortured the *compañeros* brutally, and later took them to Copala and put them in the jail. During the night these two men came back and told them they were members of the MULT and that they didn't want them back on the street again and that they were going to hang them then and there in order to put an end to all the trouble in the community. The *compañeros* began to cry — they were terrified. What's more, one of them drew a pistol and every now and then loaded it and pointed it at a *compañero*'s forehead. Afterwards they soaked the *compañeros* with cold water and later threw lime and everything on them. They were kept there for four days and three nights, and when they were released they were threatened not to tell anyone what had happened, not to create a scandal and not to become involved again with the MULT."

The state Attorney General's information disclosed no record of any formal complaint in connection with these allegations. However, it showed that on 7 May 1984 a murder inquiry was opened into the alleged killing of Juan Albino and another peasant, Juan Merino Bautista. Their bodies were discovered after they had been secretly buried, and there were said to be no witnesses to their murder. The investigation had been placed on file in the absence of witnesses able to identify those responsible.

Domingo González Domínguez and **Julio Sandoval Cruz**
Amnesty International received allegations that Domingo González Domínguez had been tortured after its mission to Mexico in January 1985. His case was described in a petition sent by members of his organization to the state Governor of Oaxaca and in reports published in the national press. Domingo González Domínguez, a MULT leader from the village of Yozoyuxi, was said to have been detained on 7 December 1984 by state police near the hamlet of Rastrojo. According to the petition, after being held in a police barracks in San Juan Copala he was transferred into the custody of the state judicial police in Putla and from there to a judicial police detention cell in Oaxaca. It was said that he was held there incommunicado for 15 days, during which time he was alleged to have been tortured both by the police and by a local civilian, alleged to have been responsible for previous abuses, including killings, in the San Juan Copala area.

Amnesty International referred to this report in a letter to the state Attorney General of Oaxaca following its mission in January 1985 and asked if any investigation had been conducted into the allegations. The letter received no reply.

Julio Sandoval Cruz, also a MULT member from Yozoyuxi, was reportedly detained by state police in his village on 13 December 1984. He was also transferred to a state judicial police cell in the city of Oaxaca, where he too was alleged to have been tortured.

Both Domingo González Domínguez and Julio Sandoval Cruz have been charged with murder, the former on multiple charges.

Paulino Martínez Delia

Paulino Martínez Delia, a bilingual teacher and MULT leader, was arrested on 24 April 1985 by municipal police in Putla. After receiving reports that he had been arrested and was being held incommunicado in a Putla police station, Amnesty International contacted the state Attorney General by telephone on 26 April and was told that Paulino Martínez was being held on several counts of murder, and that he had been visited by his family and a lawyer in the municipal prison (to which he had been transferred). Paulino Martínez subsequently told journalists that he was removed from his cell in the municipal prison in the early afternoon of 25 April by judicial police officers who hooded and handcuffed him, and took him to an unknown destination, where he was tortured with electric shocks and by having mineral water forced up his nostrils. From Paulino Martínez' own account, reported by journalists who later visited him in prison, the purpose of the interrogation was to force him to confess to a number of murders, all said to have been committed in nearby villages in the Putla district. He said that he was eventually forced to sign documents without knowing their contents, and was later returned to the municipal prison. An article on the case published in the Mexican weekly *Por Esto* included a facsimile of a medical certificate signed by a doctor who examined the prisoner on 27 April which reported sequelae which she considered had been caused by the application of electric shocks. Paulino Martínez was released in June 1985 after the charges against him were dropped. To Amnesty International's knowledge, no government investigations into allegations of torture in his case have been instituted.

****

Amnesty International found that only a small number of cases of killings and torture in the San Juan Copala region have led to the arrest and prosecution of those allegedly responsible. Of the 13 killings since the beginning of 1983, only three have resulted in arrests and criminal prosecutions. According to Amnesty International's information, in each of these cases the victims were said to be supporters of the PRI, and those arrested were leaders or members of the MULT. Most of the victims of the other 10 killings since the beginning of 1983 were said to be members of the MULT, but in these cases the investigations appear to have failed to lead to either arrest or prosecution. The information on which these figures are based is given in the cases outlined above, and in other cases summarized in Table 1.

Unfair trials

In its October 1984 memorandum Amnesty International gave details of five cases of MULT members detained on criminal charges which the organization was investigating. There were indications in each case that the indictment might be based on dubious evidence consisting in the main of uncorroborated testimony. Amnesty International was concerned that the prisoners may have been detained as a result of their political activities rather than because of any involvement in the alleged crimes. It was also concerned that given the long delays in trial proceedings noted in other cases, any irregularities or inconsistencies in the evidence which had led to their arrest might not emerge for a long time, and that, if innocent, they might therefore be subjected to an extended period of unjustified imprisonment before their eventual release.

Cases

Gregorio Martínez Cruz, Tomás Alejandro Flores and José Guadalupe de Jesús

Three local MULT leaders — Gregorio Martínez Cruz, Tomás Alejandro Flores and José Guadalupe de Jesús — were detained in October 1983 and charged with the murder of a local PRI official committed during an armed ambush near the village of Cruz Chiquita on 24 July 1983. All three denied the charges and summoned witnesses who provided them with alibis. The evidence against them appeared to be based on the statements of three of the victim's relatives who each named 22 other Triquis they claimed participated in the murder. During their mission in January 1985, the Amnesty International delegates were given the opportunity to study the court records on this case. These confirmed that the case against the three was based on evidence provided by almost identical statements from four alleged eye-witnesses, including the son, wife and brother-in-law of the victim. All claimed to have seen the defendants among a group of 25 people who each witness in turn identified by name. All 25, they claimed, had been armed and fired on the victim while they were walking in an isolated spot. Amnesty International noted that there appeared to be no evidence other than these witnesses' statements. It is highly questionable whether four separate witnesses could all actually identify the same 25 people at a distance of 30 metres in a wooded spot while an armed ambush was going on. Furthermore, one of the witnesses, during a confrontation with Gregorio Martínez Cruz, reportedly stated that he did not know him, nor had he seen him among the group allegedly responsible for the murder. In his original statement he had said that he "saw and perfectly recognized" the defendant.

Tomás Alejandro Flores was released in October 1984 after one year in prison. A federal judge granted him an appeal of *amparo* against the judge's order committing him to prison. The case against Gregorio Martínez Cruz and José Guadalupe de Jesús came to trial in May 1985, more than one and a half years after their arrest. Both prisoners were found innocent and released unconditionally.

Marcelino Guzmán Pérez

A MULT leader from the village of Río Metate, Marcelino Guzmán Pérez, was arrested on 13 October 1983 reportedly by municipal police officers from San Juan Copala accompanied by a group of armed civilians. He was said to have been severely beaten at the time of his arrest and threatened with execution by the gunmen while being taken from his village to San Juan Copala. He has been accused with six others of the murder of Francisco de Jesús Jiménez, a peasant from Cerro Cabeza, who was killed on 10 October 1983.

Information provided by the state Attorney General referred to the testimonies of three witnesses who affirmed that ''on 10 October at about 14.00 hours the accused and one other fired several shots at the victim, the firing lasted about half an hour and they knew the defendant and the others well.''

In his preparatory declaration to the judge, Marcelino Guzmán stated that at the time of the killing he was working with his farmhands in the fields and that he knew neither his accusers, nor those who had been accused with him. He told the judge that he had been beaten and threatened with death by the municipal police officers who arrested him. A witness called by the defendant to testify on his behalf said he had been employed by Marcelino Guzmán to work with him on the harvest at the time of the murder, and that he himself had witnessed the arrest and beating of the defendant while they were returning from the fields.

According to information subsequently received by Amnesty International, Marcelino Guzmán was acquitted by the court and released from prison on 27 February 1985, after spending almost one year four months in prison. The Agent of the Public Ministry appealed against the verdict and the case was referred to the State Higher Court.

Pedro Tomás Flores
Since its mission in January 1985 Amnesty International has been investigating the cases of three other Triquis arrested in 1984. They include Pedro Tomás Flores, an elderly peasant and MULT supporter, who was arrested in March 1984 on charges of wounding and murder. Amnesty International took up his case after examining the trial dossier, which indicated that there may have been a mistake over the identity of the defendant. Several witnesses called to a confrontation with the accused in the wounding case testified that Pedro Tomás Flores, who is illiterate and speaks no Spanish, was not the person cited in the prosecution's evidence. He was said to have been completely ignorant of the reasons for his arrest, which was reported to have been made without a warrant. Amnesty International noted that in the murder case, as in the 25-defendant case described above, numerous MULT leaders were identified by several alleged witnesses, all of whom made virtually identical statements. During confrontations with the accused, the witnesses ratified their previous statements, but were apparently not cross-examined.

****

As well as the cases described above, Amnesty International has received reports of the arrest of dozens of other MULT members or sympathizers in recent years, the great majority of whom have also been imprisoned on murder charges. Court documents reveal that scores of detention orders have been issued for the same offences. The information provided to Amnesty International by the state Attorney General of Oaxaca in January 1985 shows that more than 50 detention orders were issued on murder or wounding charges between April 1983 and April 1984 in the San Juan Copala area; MULT sources stated that 18 of their members or sympathizers were detained in local prisons at the beginning of 1985.

Juchitán de Zaragoza

The town of Juchitán de Zaragoza is situated close to the southern coast of the Isthmus of Tehuantepec in southeastern Oaxaca. The Zapotec Indian inhabitants of the region have retained a strong cultural identity and, in the town of Juchitán, Zapotec language and customs are still current. Since the mid-1970s political conflict in the region has intensified as a result of the growth of a left-wing grass-roots organization, the *Coalición Obrero Campesina Estudiantil del Istmo* (COCEI), the Worker-Peasant-Student Coalition of the Isthmus. Formed in 1974, the COCEI has participated actively in local politics, has pressed community claims to disputed lands which it regards as having been illegally given to private owners, and has challenged what it believes to be a lack of democracy in municipal and community affairs.

Since 1974 there have been repeated episodes of violence against COCEI members, including alleged assassinations. Armed civilians associated with local landowning and business interests and local members of the PRI were alleged to be responsible in many cases. In 1977 an army detachment previously stationed in the state of Sinaloa was brought into the area, and there were subsequent reports that COCEI members had been abducted by soldiers, and that one COCEI member had "disappeared".

In March 1981 the COCEI won municipal elections in Juchitán, in an electoral alliance with the Mexican Communist Party (PCM). Physical attacks on COCEI leaders and municipal government officials, including further assassinations and attempted assassinations, were reported following the inauguration of the COCEI municipal council. Violent clashes were also reported between supporters of the COCEI municipal government and local PRI members. The most serious of these incidents took place in Juchitán during rival electoral rallies on 31 July 1983 and resulted in the death of two people, one of them a non-participant, when violence and firing broke out. This incident led to an immediate debate in the State Legislature in Oaxaca on the disorders, and on 3 August the Legislature voted to withdraw recognition from the COCEI municipal government. Fresh municipal elections were held on 20 November and resulted in a victory for the PRI, which was, however, disputed by the COCEI.

Following the formation of the new PRI municipal government there was a sharp increase in the number of allegations that members and sympathizers of the COCEI, including prominent leaders, were the victims of human rights violations. Some abuses are alleged to have taken place in Mexico City and to have been committed by federal police officers under the jurisdiction of the federal authorities. Most of the events reported below, however, occurred in Juchitán, in the three months after 13 December 1983. On this date a large contingent of state police and troops armed with tear-gas and anti-riot weapons evicted some 90 COCEI members from the town hall of Juchitán, which they had been occupying in protest against the withdrawal of recognition from their municipal council. Eighty-six were taken prisoner and transported to Salina Cruz prison, where they were reportedly held incommunicado and in over crowded conditions for a week before most of them were released. Many were said to have been beaten at the time of arrest, and there were also reports of torture while they were being questioned by police after they had been taken into custody.

Large numbers of soldiers were stationed after this at four separate points in the town, which was heavily patrolled by units of the municipal and state preventive police, and apparently by plainclothes agents from the *Dirección Federal de Seguridad* (DFS), Federal Directorate of Security. Further clashes between police and townspeople were reported in the ensuing weeks, during which restrictions were imposed on demonstrations and political meetings. Homes were raided and numerous citizens suspected of being members or supporters of COCEI were arrested and held for questioning. There were frequent reports of beatings and torture of prisoners held in detention cells in the town hall, some of which are detailed below.

Torture and ill-treatment

In its October 1984 memorandum Amnesty International described in some detail accounts of the alleged torture and beatings of COCEI leaders and sympathizers. Some of these were publicized in national newspapers, others were documented in testimonies gathered by the organization during its research mission to Oaxaca.

Cases

Jesús Vicente Vásquez

On 15 and 16 December 1983, five COCEI leaders and sympathizers were reportedly seized by plainclothes police in Mexico City, blindfolded, and taken to a secret place of detention where they were held incommunicado for seven days and severely beaten under interrogation. Jesús Vicente Vásquez, a 30-year-old economics student and chief of the municipal police of Juchitán under the COCEI administration, was on his way to an appointment with an official of the Ministry of the Interior in Mexico City at about 9am on 15 December 1983. He is said to have been seized by plainclothes police travelling in two unmarked cars. Sabino López Aquino, a painter, and José Alfredo Hernández, a student of architecture, also COCEI members, who were accompanying him, were also seized. Reportedly, no arrest warrant was produced. The following account is based on a signed testimony by Jesús Vicente Vásquez describing his treatment while detained: he stated that he was put on the floor of the car and his head was covered with a sweater. After a short journey, he was taken inside a building where he was questioned by an officer, who accused him of several murders. He was then taken to another room where the sweater was removed from his eyes and replaced with an elastic blindfold. While in this room, he heard the voices of his friends, who were being interrogated and beaten. He was later taken before another officer and when he denied the accusations, he was taken to a downstairs room, where he was severely beaten and then left to consider his position. Over the following days, he was repeatedly beaten while being interrogated. On 21 December, he was taken before a person he thought to be a judge, while still blindfolded. A statement was drawn up which he was made to sign. He was then pushed handcuffed onto the floor of a van, driven to the airport and taken by airplane to a prison in Tehuantepec, Oaxaca. There, he was held, still blindfolded, incommunicado for three days, during two of which he was given no food. A further statement was drawn up in his presence by the Agent of the Public Ministry which he refused to sign. He was only notified of a formal order of commitment on 30 December, two weeks after his arrest.

Jesús Vicente Vásquez is currently serving a prison sentence in Tehuantepec prison after being convicted in August 1985 on multiple charges, including murder.

On the day after Jesús Vicente Vásquez' arrest, 16 December, his wife, Bertha Ovalle Bustos, and another COCEI leader, Juan López López, were reportedly abducted in a similar fashion in Mexico City and taken to the same prison. Juan López López told Amnesty International that he too was blindfolded and beaten. His account of his interrogation and beating by the police is similar to that of Jesús Vicente Vásquez. On 22 December, Sabino López Aquino, José Alfredo Hernández, Bertha Ovalle Bustos and Juan López López were released. Juan López López told Amnesty International that his hearing was impaired as a result of blows received during his interrogation. Jesús Vicente Vásquez stated that the beatings he received caused broken ribs and an injured spine.

In the legal information provided by the state Attorney General of Oaxaca on the case of Jesús Vicente Vásquez in January 1985, the date given for the issue of a formal remand order against him was 27 December 1983, 12 days after his reported arrest in Mexico City. Since the Mexican Constitution allows only for a period of three days during which a person may be detained without the issue of a formal remand order, it would appear that for at least a week, during which he was being held incommunicado for interrogation, his detention was illegal and unconstitutional. Nevertheless, there was no indication in the official information on this case that any investigation had been conducted into the reported irregularity of the detention, or into the allegations of ill-treatment.

Rosalino Vásquez López, Miguel Guerra Vásquez and José Cruz Jiménez
Rosalino Vásquez López, a metalworker, Miguel Guerra Vásquez, a

firework-maker and José Cruz Jiménez, a peasant, were arrested by municipal police in Juchitán on 1 January 1984. On that day a protest meeting held by COCEI in the streets of Juchitán led to a violent clash with a contingent of PRI supporters in which shots were fired, buildings were burned and a number of people were seriously injured. After their arrest, the three were taken to the town hall where they were apparently held incommunicado for eight days. Although they were known to be in custody because their arrest took place in public, the authorities allegedly denied that they were in detention and deliberately misled relatives seeking information as to their whereabouts. Despite inquiries the relatives were unable to find out which authority was responsible for their arrest or custody. While being held incommunicado they were said to have been badly beaten by members of the state preventive police, denied access to legal assistance and medical attention, and forced to sign statements prepared beforehand which they were not allowed to read. It was alleged that while they were being held incommunicado in Juchitán town hall, two prominent local civilian members of the PRI participated in their interrogation and threatened them. They were later moved to the municipal prison where their relatives were allowed to see them for the first time on 9 January (eight days after their arrest). Rosalino Vásquez was said to have been severely bruised around the face and on the ribs, and Miguel Guerra Vásquez to have wounds on his head, apparently caused by blows from a stick or truncheon.

Information provided by the state Attorney General of Oaxaca on these cases shows that they were committed for trial on 7 January 1984 on charges of provoking a crime, criminal association, grievous attack, robbery and damage to property. The offences were said to have been committed during the disorder on 1 January. They appeared before the judge for the first time on 10 January, and retracted their confessions. A formal order of custody was not made by the judge until 11 January, 10 days after their arrest. They were released on 2 June 1984 after an *amparo* petition, filed on their behalf against the formal custody order, was granted by the court. Although the municipal authorities may hold someone in preventive custody for a period not exceeding 24 hours, in this case the prisoners appear to have been held incommunicado for more than seven days before their families or a lawyer were able to see them, and for six days before their case was presented to a judge.

David Cruz Velásquez and **Hermila Guerra López**
David Cruz Velásquez, a 19-year-old engineering student, and Hermila Guerra López, both COCEI supporters, were arrested by an officer of the state preventive police at about 8pm on 1 January 1984,

while they were visiting a sick friend in hospital in Juchitán. The police had apparently entered the hospital in order to identify and interview individuals wounded during the COCEI demonstration earlier that day. They were taken together by police car to a police station, where, according to the testimony of both prisoners, they were tortured by being beaten, by being made to stand for long periods against a wall in a cruciform position, and by being given electric shocks. They were pressed to admit to being members of COCEI and to involvement in acts of violence on 1 January. They denied the accusations. On 4 January they were moved to the municipal prison of Juchitán. On 11 January the court of first instance of Juchitán ordered their release for lack of evidence and on 13 January they were released.

In this case too the prisoners appear to have been detained without an arrest order and to have been held incommunicado for nearly a week before their case was brought before a judge.

****

During January and February 1984 suspected COCEI supporters were repeatedly arrested by the municipal police backed by state preventive police patrols. Many of these arrests appear to have been made without lawful authority or reasonable cause. COCEI members state that there were on average four arrests a week during this two-month period. The detainees were normally held for several days in cells in the town hall where many were alleged to have been beaten and ill-treated before they were released, often only after paying a summary fine to the municipal authorities. The Mexican press continued to report such cases, although fewer of them, later in 1984.

Political killings and "disappearances"

Since its formation in 1974, more than 20 COCEI supporters are reported to have been killed, apparently as a result of intense local opposition to the movement's policies. Since its electoral victory in 1981, there have been reports of unprovoked attacks on officials of the COCEI municipal government and COCEI supporters by armed civilians said to be local PRI members or acting at their instigation. Although detailed information on earlier reported killings of COCEI members is not available, reports of recent incidents suggest that in the majority of cases, the alleged culprits have not been vigorously pursued or prosecuted by the authorities.

Víctor Pineda Henestrosa

Amnesty International is still concerned about the failure of the authorities to carry out a satisfactory investigation into the "disappearance" of Víctor Pineda Henestrosa, a primary school teacher and land official. He was reported to have been seized on 11 July 1978 in the centre of Juchitán by a group of armed individuals, four of whom were reported by witnesses to have been in army uniforms. According to statements signed before the Agent of the Public Ministry of Juchitán in September 1979 by Cándida Santiago Jiménez, his wife, and three other witnesses, he was seized from his car near the Juchitán bus station at about 10am on the morning of 11 July 1978. Acording to the witnesses a van pulled up beside his red Volkswagen and six men with rifles got out, seized him, pushed him into their van and drove off. Two of the men were said to be in civilian clothes and the other four in military uniform. One of the uniformed men, said to be an inhabitant of Juchitán, was named by all three witnesses in their statements. Víctor Pineda Henestrosa, a member of the teachers' trade union as well as an active COCEI member, had previously been working as a local official of the Ministry of Land Reform in Juchitán. At the time of his "disappearance" he was an advisor to the *comisariado de bienes comunales*, Commissioner of communal lands. He was known to have helped peasants and workers to resolve agrarian and labour problems. His alleged abduction took place shortly before elections for the post of *Comisariado*, Commissioner.

No written details on this case were included in the information provided to the Amnesty International delegates by the state Attorney General. However, during a meeting in January 1985 the Attorney General told Amnesty International that the state Attorney General's office had no record of the case, and that no formal complaint had been made to the authorities. On 11 March Amnesty International raised the case again in a letter to the Attorney General, appending a copy of the witnesses' statement to the Agent of the Public Ministry, together with a statement signed by the Agent certifying that the copy was a faithful reproduction of the original held in the files of the Attorney General's office. No reply was received to this letter. Other information received by Amnesty International concerning this case indicates that it was presented on several occe "ions to federal government and military authorities. However, it would appear that neither the state nor the federal authorities have satisfactorily clarified the whereabouts or fate of Víctor Pineda Henestrosa. It also appears that a proper investigation has never been conducted into the evidence presented by the witnesses to his abduction. The failure of the state authorities to provide any information on this case was surprising in view of the fact that it is well-known locally and that the COCEI appears to have continuously pressed the state authorities for a full

54

investigation. Members of the 11th Army Battalion stationed at the time in the neighbouring town of Ixtepec are alleged to have been responsible for the illegal detention and subsequent "disappearance" of Víctor Pineda Henestrosa. The same unit was said to have been responsible for the abduction in January 1978 of COCEI leader Leopoldo de Gyves Pineda, an army officer who was subsequently imprisoned in Mexico City on multiple charges related to his political activities (see below).

Imprisonment of COCEI leaders

During its January 1985 mission Amnesty International expressed concern about the continued imprisonment of Jesús Vicente Vásquez, Leopoldo de Gyves Pineda, Carlos Sánchez López and Manuel Vásquez Nicolás, who were arrested in December 1983 and at the time of the mission were awaiting trial in a prison in Tehuantepec, Oaxaca. All four men are COCEI leaders or were officials in the COCEI municipal council of Juchitán from 1981 to 1983. Amnesty International was concerned that the criminal charges against them appeared to be based on weak or questionable evidence and that they may in fact have been imprisoned as a result of their non-violent activities as members of the COCEI and of the municipal government of Juchitán.

Cases

Carlos Sánchez López, Leopoldo de Gyves Pineda and Manuel Vásquez Nicolás

Carlos Sánchez López, Leopoldo de Gyves Pineda and Manuel Vásquez Nicolás were arrested on 13 December 1983 while taking part in the occupation of the Juchitán town hall. Carlos Sánchez López, a founding member of COCEI, is a 36-year-old industrial mechanic and a leader of the *Central de Trabajadores del Istmo* (CTI), Union of Workers of the Isthmus, a COCEI-affiliated trade union. Leopoldo de Gyves Pineda, a 64-year-old retired army major, is the father of the municipal president of Juchitán during the 1981 to 1983 administration. He was a founding member of COCEI and has himself stood twice as an independent candidate in municipal elections. In 1978 he was abducted by troops and later sentenced by a military tribunal to three and a half years' imprisonment on multiple charges under the military and common penal codes relating to his political activities. He served the sentence in *Campo Militar No.1*, Military Camp No.1, in Mexico City. Manuel Vásquez Nicolás, a 46-year-old carpenter, was active during the COCEI administration in Juchitán as a community leader.

After their arrest the three were remanded in custody to await trial in the prison of Salina Cruz, Oaxaca, on several charges of damage to property, carrying prohibited weapons, obstruction, criminal association, offences against public servants, instigation to commit a crime and plunder. They denied the charges and appealed against the order remanding them in custody. In August 1984 they were additionally charged with murder, wounding and firing a gun — the same offences alleged to have been committed by Jesús Vicente Vásquez (see below) during a political rally in Juchitán on 31 July 1983. In September 1984 they applied for bail which was fixed at 100,000 pesos (US$880). They were absolved when their case came to trial, and released on 16 August 1985.

Jesús Vicente Vásquez
Jesús Vicente Vásquez, a 30-year-old economics student and former chief of the Juchitán municipal police, was arrested in Mexico City on 15 December 1983 (see Chapter II). He was being held, as of October 1985, in a prison in Tehuantepec, Oaxaca, after being sentenced in August 1985 to 10 years six months' imprisonment on charges of plunder, obstruction, provocation of a crime and criminal association, offences against public servants and threatening behaviour. He had also been accused of murder and wounding in connection with a shooting in Juchitán on 31 July 1983.

In May 1984, Amnesty International adopted all four of these as prisoners of conscience. The organization believed that the charges against them resulted from demands made by the COCEI municipal council over rights to land, legal problems of demarcation and rights of way, which brought them into conflict with local vested interests, prominent local members of the PRI and the state authorities. The charges of violence against them arose from an incident which took place in the centre of Juchitán on 31 July 1983, during rival electoral rallies organized by the COCEI and the PRI at the close of campaigns for the election of local deputies to the state assembly. Two people — Miguel López Posadas, an ice-seller and COCEI supporter, and Isidro Pineda Orozco, a PRI supporter — were killed and more than 20 others injured when shooting broke out during a clash between the two parties.

There were serious contradictions between the official view of the incident and that of the COCEI. The COCEI maintains that local PRI leaders and supporters deliberately attempted to provoke a violent clash. Eye-witnesses attested to having seen several known local PRI leaders firing on the crowd from behind cover, some of them from the roofs of nearby buildings. The autopsy results reportedly confirmed that both victims had been shot from above. In addition, despite the presence of a large contingent of state preventive police in the town, they allegedly failed to intervene to stop the violence or to arrest any of the armed civilians said to have been involved. Three days later, on 3 August, the Oaxaca State Parliament voted to withdraw recognition from the COCEI municipal council, accusing it of direct responsibility for the violence and of failure to maintain order in the city.

During its mission of January 1985, Amnesty International was able to discuss the incident in greater detail with state government authorities, who repeated the official view that COCEI members started the incident and opened fire on a peaceful procession of PRI supporters. The state government told the Amnesty International delegation that television film existed showing Jesús Vicente Vásquez and others firing on other people. Amnesty International has not seen this film.

The COCEI version seems to be strengthened by reports of a series of similar incidents in 1982 and 1983, when COCEI members allege that local PRI members repeatedly provoked violent incidents resulting on more than one occasion in deaths. However, in these cases too, the authorities' view appears to have been that responsibility for the disorders lay with the COCEI leadership.

Photocopy of a formal declaration about the "disappearance" of Víctor Pineda Henestrosa on 11 July 1978. This statement was made to the Agent of the Public Ministry in Juchitán by the victim's wife, Cándida Santiago Jiménez. The handwritten note at the top of the document gives the number of the official inquiry (*averiguación previa* No.388/79). A copy of this document was sent to the Oaxaca state government by Amnesty International in March 1985, but the authorities provided no details of any investigation in their official reply to Amnesty International in January 1986.

In her statement Cándida Santiago Jiménez names one of the alleged kidnappers of her husband, whom she claims was a soldier stationed at a military base at Ixtepec. He was named in statements to the Public Ministry by other witnesses.

There has been no official word on the fate and whereabouts of Víctor Pineda Henestrosa since July 1978.

58

San Juan Copala — a remote town in the state of Oaxaca, in the rural southeast of
Mexico.

Army troops on patrol, San Juan Copala. During the early 1980s soldiers stationed in
the town were among those alleged to be responsible for abuses, including beatings and
torture of villagers.

A rally during municipal elections in San Juan Copala, Oaxaca, December 1982.

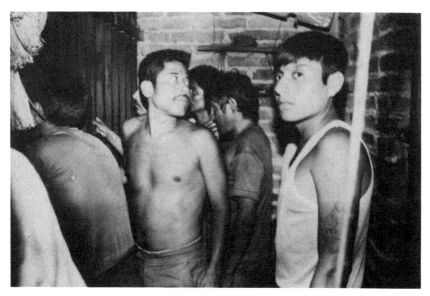

Triqui prisoners in the municipal prison of Putla, state of Oaxaca.

60

A rally of supporters of the *Coalición Obrero Campesina Estudiantil del Istmo* (COCEI), Worker-Peasant-Student Coalition of the Isthmus, in Juchitán. The building in the background is a public library which was renamed by the COCEI municipal council after Víctor Pineda Henestrosa, a local leader who "disappeared" after his detention on 11 July 1978.

61

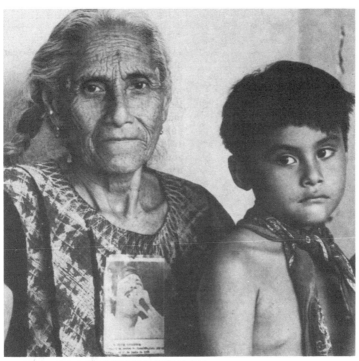

The mother of Víctor Pineda Henestrosa, pictured with one of his two children. She wears his photograph, bearing the caption: "Víctor Pineda Henestrosa, detained in the centre of Juchitán, Oaxaca, by the army, 11 July 1978". Víctor Pineda Henestrosa was a member of a teachers' trade union and an active supporter of the COCEI, advising peasants and workers on agrarian and labour problems. Four of the six armed men who seized him were wearing military uniforms, according to witnesses.

Víctor Pineda Henestrosa

62

Leopoldo de Gyves Pineda, a 66-year-old former army major and a founder member of the COCEI. He was detained in Juchitán on 15 December 1983 and indicted on multiple charges arising out of political disturbances in Juchitán. In 1978 he had been abducted by troops and later sentenced by a military tribunal to three and a half years' imprisonment on charges relating to his political activities. Amnesty International considered the charges involving violence to be unfounded and adopted him as a prisoner of conscience following its March 1984 mission, when a delegate interviewed him in prison in Salina Cruz. He was acquitted by the court and released on 16 August 1985.

Carlos Sánchez López, an industrial mechanic, founder member of the COCEI, and leader of the COCEI affiliated trade union *Central de Trabajadores del Istmo*, Union of Workers of the Isthmus. He was detained with Leopoldo de Gyves Pineda in December 1983. He was adopted by Amnesty International as a prisoner of conscience, and was released in August 1985 when the case came to trial. He too was charged with damage to property, carrying prohibited weapons, obstruction, criminal association, offences against public servants, instigation of crime and plunder. In August 1984 he was additionally charged with murder, wounding and firing a gun, after disturbances during a political rally in Juchitán in July 1983.

Manuel Vázquez Nicolás, a carpenter and COCEI leader in Juchitán. Together with Leopoldo de Gyves Pineda and Carlos Sánchez López he was arrested on 13 December 1983 and charged with multiple offences, including criminal association and plunder. All three were closely associated with the COCEI municipal council which administered Juchitán from 1981 to 1983. In August 1984 they were additionally charged with murder, wounding and firing a gun — the same offences alleged to have been committed by Jesús Vicente Vásquez *(below)*. Believing the charges to be unfounded, Amnesty International adopted him as a prisoner of conscience and worked for his release. He was acquitted and released when his case came to trial on 16 August 1985.

Jesús Vicente Vásquez, a 32-year-old economics student and former commander of the municipal police in Juchitán. He was detained on 15 December 1983 by plainclothes police in Mexico City and held incommunicado for two days before a formal custody order was issued. During this time he claimed to have been severely beaten while under interrogation. He was subsequently charged with responsibility for the killing of two participants in a political rally in Juchitán in July 1983. Believing these charges to be unfounded, Amnesty International adopted him as a prisoner of conscience. In August 1985 he was sentenced to 10 years six months' imprisonment. The Oaxaca state authorities have denied allegations that he was ill-treated.

CHAPTER III

Evidence of abuses in the state of Chiapas

The Amnesty International mission of March 1984 visited two regions of rural Chiapas — the Simojovel region in the northern part of the state and the Central Highlands region (*Los Altos*) — to investigate reports of human rights abuses including alleged political killings and torture. This chapter deals with specific incidents about which information was collected during the mission and which were later submitted as evidence to the Government of Mexico in Amnesty International's October 1984 memorandum. As in the previous chapter on the state of Oaxaca, reference is also made to official information on cases made available by the state Attorney General to the Amnesty International delegation which visited the state capital, Tuxtla Gutiérrez, from 31 January to 2 February 1985. Some additional cases are included which have been reported since the mission and on which representatives of the state government have not, therefore, had the opportunity to comment.

Political killings

In its October 1984 memorandum Amnesty International documented in detail a number of incidents in the Simojovel region in which peasants were allegedly beaten and shot in what appeared to be deliberate attacks by landlords and detachments of state security police on peasants involved in land or labour disputes. Many of those said to have been affected were tied agricultural workers on privately owned coffee-farms, and, in particular, members of an independent trade union, the *Central Independiente de Obreros Agrícolas y Campesinas* (CIOAC), Independent Union of Agricultural Workers and Peasants. Amnesty International's concern in these cases was that peasants, including women and children, appeared to have been shot at and ill-treated repeatedly during attempts to evict them from land. In one such incident which took place on the *ejidos* La Pimienta and Yotolchén on 11 April 1984, two peasants belonging to the *Confederación Nacional Campesina* (CNC), National Peasant Confederation, were shot dead by state security police allegedly accompanied by local landowners during an altercation between the peasants and the police.

Amnesty International has studied the information provided by the state Attorney General on the results of official investigations of these incidents. This confirmed reports of injuries sustained by peasants in a number of cases. However, the circumstances of the incidents did not suggest that there had been deliberate attempts to kill selected peasants, nor that there had been a deliberate policy of carrying out or permitting killings.

A pattern of apparently deliberate political killings was, however, observed by Amnesty International in the Central Highlands region and particularly in the municipal districts of Venustiano Carranza and Villa de las Rosas. The majority of the reported victims were supporters of independent peasant organizations or rural trade unions. The killings appear to have occurred in nearly all cases in the context of long-standing land disputes. However, there were no indications — either from independent sources or from information provided by the judicial authorities — that members of the official security forces had been involved. In all cases the killings were apparently carried out by civilians. Amnesty International's concern arose from repeated allegations that the killings had taken place at the instigation of, or with the consent of, local municipal authorities, and that the state authorities had not brought those responsible to justice.

The rural community of Venustiano Carranza has been divided for many years as a result of a conflict over 3,200 hectares of fertile land in private ownership. Community members claim this land was included in a presidential resolution of 1965 which conferred on the villagers title to communal lands. A further source of conflict has been the alleged failure of the authorities to compensate the community in full for lands flooded as a result of the construction of a reservoir in La Angostura. Disagreement over these demands has led to long-standing political divisions within the community itself between a faction loyal to the ruling political party, the PRI, and an opposition group, who are supporters of the *Organización Campesina Emiliano Zapata* (OCEZ), the Emiliano Zapata Peasant Organization. Leaders of this group list 15 community activists and sympathizers who they say have been assassinated by armed civilians between 1967 and 1981. They claim that local landowners, in collusion with the municipal authorities, were responsible for instigating the killings and that most of the killings were carried out by armed civilians loyal to the official peasant organization, the CNC. During the 1970s these divisions within the community caused repeated violent incidents leading to intervention by the army and the arrest and prosecution of community leaders on serious criminal charges. However, the assassination of community leaders or peasants belonging to the OCEZ rarely if ever led to arrests or prosecution, according to OCEZ leaders. Killings were also reported in the nearby town of Villa de las Rosas in incidents which appeared to be related to a long-standing dispute over the ownership of *ejidal* lands in San Isidro La Cuchilla. The victims were said to be members or supporters of the CIOAC. Other villagers belonged to an opposing group led by the CNC.

In its October 1984 memorandum Amnesty International documented eight such killings, which reportedly occurred between 1966 and 1982 in Venustiano Carranza and Villa de las Rosas. All eight victims were said to be either community leaders active in efforts to recover or regularize communal or *ejidal* lands, or supporters of opposition peasant organizations. Representatives of the peasant organizations to which the victims belonged maintained that in all cases, armed civilians were responsible, acting in association with private landowners and with the complicity or acquiescence of municipal authorities. Although Amnesty International cannot substantiate such an allegation directly, it noted that of the five cases in which murder investigations had been opened, only in one case was anyone brought to trial. Even in this case, those accused were absolved and released by a local judge and were never rearrested, despite a High Court decision reversing the judge's verdict and sentencing them to prison.

A summary of the reported circumstances of these killings and of the results of criminal investigations initiated by local offices of the Public Ministry is given in Table 2.

Cases

Elpidio Vásquez Vásquez

Elpidio Vásquez Vásquez, a CIOAC member, was shot dead by an unknown assailant in the centre of Villa de las Rosas at about 11pm on 9 September 1979 according to the testimony of an eye-witness, who was wounded in the attack. The assailants were said to have arrived outside the home of another peasant, Eliezar Grajales, in a municipal truck and to have opened fire deliberately on him and his companions, killing Elpidio Vásquez Vásquez instantly. Two people — Rodrigo Ordoñez Santiago, the municipal president of Villa de las Rosas, and Librado Arguello — were said to have been arrested after the killing, but were released after a few days. This case, which was not included in Amnesty International's October 1984 memorandum, was subsequently raised by Amnesty International in a letter sent to the state Attorney General in March 1985. Although no reply had been received to its March letter at the time of writing (October 1985), Amnesty International does not believe anyone has been brought to trial in connection with this killing.

Tzacacum, Chalchihuitán

In its October 1984 memorandum Amnesty International described an incident in the village of Tzacacum, Chalchihuitán, in the Los Altos region of Chiapas. Eleven peasants, some of them young children, were reportedly killed and others wounded when a group of armed civilians attacked their village early in the morning of 24 March 1983, setting fire to their homes and gunning them down as they tried to escape. According to press reports published at the time, the attack resulted from a long-standing conflict between the villagers and a group of local landowners, closely associated with the municipal authorities of Chalchihuitán. The municipal authorities were said to have systematically ill-treated villagers and to have evicted them if they refused to comply with demands for weekly payments. Some of the dissident villagers were said to have been pursuing legal channels in an attempt to separate themselves from the municipality. The attack was said to have been planned as a reprisal against this group by local landowners in association with the municipal authorities. These allegations prompted a swift investigation by the state authorities of Chiapas which led to the arrest of more than 15 people, among them the then municipal president of Chalchihuitán, Nicolás López Gómez, and other local officials. However, those interviewed about the incident by Amnesty International delegates in March 1984 maintained that other prominent local leaders alleged to be jointly responsible had evaded arrest, despite the issue of arrest warrants against them. Although no written details of this incident were provided by the authorities during the 1985 Amnesty International mission, the state Attorney General confirmed orally the arrests made as a result of the criminal investigation. The Amnesty International delegates were unable to obtain official confirmation that local government officials had been found criminally responsible for the killings, which were described by state government officials as the result of a violent clash between *indígenas*, Indians.

****

During 1984, following its mission in March, Amnesty International received further reports of violent attacks on supporters of independent peasant organizations (particularly OCEZ and CIOAC) in the Los Altos region of Chiapas. In common with the cases already described, members of the official security forces do not appear to have been involved. Those allegedly responsible were armed civilians, often said to be members of the CNC or gunmen apparently acting in association with local landowners.

Andrés Domínguez Rodríguez and José Rodríguez Mendoza
At about 11am on 27 July 1984 an attempt was made on the life of
José Rodríguez Mendoza, a caneworkers' leader and a leading
member of the *Unión de Ejidos 28 de setiembre*, 28 September
Union of *Ejidos*. The van in which he was travelling was reportedly
ambushed by gunmen near the "El Coyol" ranch on the road between
Pujiltic and Villa de las Rosas, in Venustiano Carranza. Andrés
Domínguez Rodríguez,a Guatemalan peasant who was a passenger
in the vehicle, was shot and killed, and José Rodríguez was seriously
injured with multiple bullet wounds. As far as Amnesty International
is aware, the investigation into the incident has not yet led to the
identification of those responsible.

Domingo Calvo Espinosa and eight others
At about 7pm on 6 October 1984 a group of 17 peasants from Venustiano Carranza belonging to the OCEZ were reportedly ambushed in
their truck while travelling to help their colleagues whose vehicle had
run out of petrol at El Roblar ranch, near Venustiano Carranza. On
arriving at the stranded vehicle the peasants were reportedly attacked
by a group of about a hundred peasants armed with shotguns travelling in three trucks. Although unarmed they were reportedly fired on
indiscriminately, leaving nine dead, including Bartolo Ramírez Pérez,
who was only 12 years old, and four seriously wounded. Three
members of the group, including the driver of their vehicle, were
abducted by the armed men and handed over to local police, but
were later released. The assailants in this case were reported
to be members of a CNC group opposed to the OCEZ known
locally as *Los Paraiseños*. The motive for the attack appeared
to be revenge following the assassination of their leader, Bartolo
Gómez, a CNC official. They apparently believed that the OCEZ
were responsible for the killing. OCEZ leaders rejected this accusation and themselves accused local landowners of planning and carrying it out as a means of frustrating an imminent agreement between the two rival factions of the community. State officials
commenting orally on the killings told the Amnesty International
delegates that a swift investigation had been conducted and that 13
CNC peasants had been detained a few days after the incident.
However, in August 1985 it was reported in the press that 12 of those
detained had been released. According to the reports, the 12 had
been sentenced to four years' imprisonment for group homicide, but
were subsequently released on bail. The state penal code in force at
the time of the trial prescribed a sentence of 10 to 20 years' imprisonment for the offence of intentional homicide. The lower sentence and
early release of the prisoners was due, according to the authorities, to

the impossibility of attributing individual responsibility to the accused.

Juan Gómez Cruz and **Leandro García López**

Juan Gómez Cruz, Municipal Agent of the village of Ostuacán and a member of the OCEZ, is reported to have been shot dead in the street on the night of 22 December 1984 in the Colonia Lindavista. The OCEZ accused a group of CNC cattlemen who had been denied grazing rights on *ejidal* lands. On the following day, the same group were reported to have attacked with machetes and seriously wounded another peasant belonging to the OCEZ, Leandro García López. A formal complaint naming those allegedly responsible was registered with the Agent of the Public Ministry, but to Amnesty International's knowledge the investigation into the killings has not led to any arrests.

Enrique Vásquez Hernández and **Alejandro Aguilar Pérez**

CNC members were also among those allegedly responsible for an armed ambush on Enrique Vásquez Hernández and Alejandro Aguilar Pérez, both members of the regional committee of CIOAC in the district of Las Margaritas. The attack is said to have taken place at about 9.30pm on 27 January 1985 when Enrique Vásquez and Alejandro Aguilar were returning from a meeting in the *Ejido La Unión de Uniones,* the *Ejido* Union of Unions. The van in which they were travelling is reported to have been fired on repeatedly, and Enrique Vásquez was hit in the shoulder by a bullet. As in other incidents, the attack appears to have resulted from hostility between the CNC and CIOAC over the use of *ejidal* property. A formal complaint was made to the Agent of the Public Ministry naming six individuals, including three local CNC leaders and a local landowner, who were said to have been clearly identified. Amnesty International does not know of any arrests in this case although arrest orders were reportedly issued by a court.

Further killings and attempted killings of CIOAC leaders in Las Margaritas were reported in August and October 1985. All of the victims were close political colleagues working with *ejidos* in the Las Margaritas district; reportedly some had been attacked on several occasions or subjected to death threats. In three of the incidents the same person — reportedly a paid gunman — was among those alleged to be responsible.

On 6 August 1985 Gregorio López Aguilar, an official of the *ejido* Las Margaritas and a local CIOAC leader, was killed. A CNC official of a neighbouring *ejido* was formally denounced as being responsible for the killing. Two other CIOAC members — Hilario Jiménez López and Ajilio Trejo Jiménez — were taken to hospital with bullet wounds. According to press reports, an official of the state Attorney

General's office told journalists that the killing had arisen from a personal dispute between the four peasants. Preliminary investigations had established that the alleged attacker had acted in self-defence after being assaulted himself, the official said, nevertheless adding that orders for his arrest had been issued.

According to Amnesty International's information this person was one of those accused of attempting to assassinate Enrique Vásquez and Alejandro Aguilar the previous January. Although an order for his arrest had been issued by a court after the assassination attempt, the police authority reportedly failed to take steps to apprehend him. In the subsequent months from February until October 1985 four other CIOAC leaders were reportedly the targets of similar attacks.

According to press reports, peasants of the *ejido* Las Margaritas were pressing for title to 150 hectares of land which is currently under private tenure. As a result, a conflict had reportedly arisen between the peasants and the landowner, who is a close relative of the State Governor. It was also reported that a CIOAC demand for a revision of boundaries had met strong opposition from a rival group of land claimants led by the CNC.

Andulio Gálvez Velásquez
On 4 October 1985 at about 7pm, four gunmen travelling in a green Volkswagen car shot and killed Andulio Gálvez Velásquez, a lawyer and Education Secretary with the CIOAC State Committee in Chiapas. Andulio Gálvez, who was a PSUM (Unified Socialist Party of Mexico) candidate for elections to the State Congress, was well known locally for his legal work on behalf of peasants detained on land-related offences, and for his legal assistance to peasant groups including the *ejidatarios* of Las Margaritas. He was one of several lawyers interviewed by Amnesty International during its March 1984 mission to Chiapas. Andulio Gálvez was shot repeatedly outside his office (a rural credit organization) in the centre of Comitán. The killing, which appeared to have been carefully planned, followed a number of previous attempts. According to reports, both his home and that of Enrique Vásquez Hernández had been raided by gunmen the previous August; neither of them were home at the time. In the following months Andulio Gálvez and other CIOAC leaders were reported to have received repeated death threats.

On the day after the killing of Andulio Gálvez, members of the state judicial police allegedly tortured two other employees of the credit organization for which he had worked, apparently in an attempt to incriminate members in the killing. On 5 October two members of the CIOAC Comitán branch — Felipe de Jesús Santis and Eleazar

Velasco, both close colleagues of Andulio Gálvez — were detained apparently without warrant in Comitán by state judicial police. They alleged that they had been blindfolded and taken to a place they could not identify. There they were reportedly tortured in an attempt to force them to sign a document giving details of "internal divisions" within the union. A press article which appeared subsequently quoted an official of the state Attorney General's office as saying that Andulio Gálvez' death had been provoked by disputes within the union, an allegation which union officials denied. The two men were reportedly held for 48 hours and then released.

Two of the people alleged to have shot Andulio Gálvez were later reportedly detained. Both were reported to be members of the CNC. Warrants were also reportedly issued for the arrest of the other two, who included the CNC official accused of killing Gregorio López. At the time of writing (October 1985), Amnesty International had not been able to obtain official confirmation of the arrests or of the charges on which the men were being held.

Torture and ill-treatment: prisoners of conscience

During 1982 and 1983 Amnesty International was concerned about a number of reports of torture inflicted on detainees by state judicial police officers. Press accounts and individual testimonies also reported routine ill-treatment, particularly beatings, of peasants at the moment of their arrest. There were a number of detailed reports of prisoners being tortured while held incommunicado for police interrogation on the premises of the Attorney General's headquarters in the state capital, Tuxtla Gutiérrez. Some of these prisoners appeared to have been detained without a legal warrant and without any official acknowledgement of their arrest or place of detention. The allegations include the use of physical torture — such as electric shocks, the forcing of mineral water up the nostrils, and beatings — and psychological pressure, such as death threats against detainees and their families. Torture is alleged to have been used to obtain incriminating statements from suspects. During initial police interrogation detainees do not have access to legal counsel.

Amnesty International has adopted as prisoners of conscience three prisoners held in Chiapas. Each has been convicted of criminal offences, but Amnesty International believes they are actually imprisoned on account of their non-violent political activities. Each of the prisoners has alleged ill-treatment under police interrogation. These allegations have not, to Amnesty International's knowledge, been investigated.

Cases

Gustavo Zárate Vargas
Gustavo Zárate Vargas, a 30-year-old economics teacher at the Autonomous University of Chiapas in San Cristóbal de las Casas, was seized by plainclothes members of the state judicial police at about 12pm on 24 July 1983 in San Cristóbal de las Casas. Before his arrest, while coordinator of the university social sciences faculty in 1982, he played an active part in a campaign for internal reform in the university. He had also taken part in a campaign for the reinstatement of a group of workers who had been dismissed from the *Instituto Nacional Indigenista*, the National Institute for Indigenous Peoples. He was known to have worked to promote the welfare of Guatemalan refugees in Chiapas and to have been an active supporter of Indian communities involved in land disputes in the region. He was a member of the *Partido Revolucionario de los Trabajadores* (PRT), Workers' Revolutionary Party, a legally registered political party in Mexico which has participated in national and state elections.

After he had been formally committed to prison to await trial, he publicized details of his alleged illegal arrest and torture, accounts of which were published in the national press. He also submitted a formal appeal against the custody order on 4 August 1983 to the First District Judge of Tuxtla Gutiérrez. In his statement to the judge, he said that no arrest warrant was produced by those who arrested him, and that his house was searched later on the same day without authority. He stated that from 9pm on the day of his arrest to 5am on 25 July, and on repeated occasions over the next two days, he was tortured: beaten on the body and the head while blindfolded, and had mineral water forced up his nostrils. He said he was threatened with execution if he refused to agree to the accusations of the police interrogators. Gustavo Zárate was interviewed in Cerro Hueco prison in March 1984 by an Amnesty International representative. During the interview he confirmed his previous statement and told the Amnesty International representative that the torture included the application of electricity to his nose, ears and genitals and beatings on his stomach with a soaked towel. He said he was forced to sign a statement which he was not allowed to read and was threatened with execution if he failed to do so.

The documents provided to Amnesty International reveal that he was interrogated at length about his political activities and connections, and that at the same time two university students were also being held without warrant and subjected to similar interrogations. He told the judge that the police had accused him of holding suspicious meetings with foreigners in his home, an accusation based on statements alleged to have been made to the police by neighbours. The neighbours, who reportedly claimed that weapons and drugs were being stored in his home, were never called to testify in the trial. After his arrest, his home was searched. The police removed political books and pamphlets, but he was later charged with possession of marijuana and weapons, including a pistol and home-made bombs which the police claimed to have discovered during the search.

After studying the available court documents and other information relating to the circumstances of his arrest and the political background of the case, Amnesty International concluded that there were strong indications that he had been the victim of a deliberate frame-up. Amnesty International believed that he had been imprisoned because of his non-violent political activities and adopted him as a prisoner of conscience. In reaching this decision, Amnesty International took into account the fact that he had been arrested illegally and held incommunicado for several days without access to his family or a lawyer, while being interrogated mainly about his political activities; that there were strong indications that he had been convicted on the basis of a coerced confession, which he later retracted and which he said he had been forced to sign under torture; and that there were well-founded reasons for doubting the credibility of the alleged discovery of drugs and weapons in his home.

Since the possession of illegal drugs and weapons are offences under federal jurisdiction, his case was handed over to the Federal Public Ministry who charged him under the *Ley Federal de Armas y Explosivos*, the Federal Law of Arms and Explosives. On 5 December 1983 he was convicted and sentenced to eight years' imprisonment. This was reduced on appeal to seven years three months on 27 January 1984. In March 1984 he lodged an *amparo* appeal against the sentence with the *Suprema Corte de la Nación*, the Supreme Court of the Nation. On 23 November 1984 the Supreme Court acceded to his appeal for *amparo*, finding several irregularities in the trial proceedings against him, and his sentence was reduced to two years three months. He was released on 1 March 1985 on payment of a fine of 5,200 pesos and bail of 100,000 pesos (approximately US$880).

During their meeting with the state Attorney General of Chiapas in January 1985, the Amnesty International mission delegates were given full access to the court documents pertaining to the case of Gustavo Zárate. The court record clearly disclosed the existence of a complaint alleging that he had been tortured. While the judge to whom the complaint was addressed appears to have rejected his appeal against the custody order, no investigation was carried out into the allegations that he had been tortured. In commenting on the case, the state Attorney General pointed out that the investigation of an alleged offence would proceed as a matter of course after the presentation of a formal complaint to the Agent of the Public Ministry, who is empowered to conduct such investigations on behalf of the Attorney General. No formal complaint had been presented to the Agent of the Public Ministry in this case or in any of the other cases of alleged torture raised by Amnesty International. He said that because no such formal complaints had been made, there had in recent years been no grounds for investigations or proceedings against police officers accused of abuses against detainees.

Amnesty International believes that the allegations set out above, some of which were disclosed in the court records, were sufficiently credible to have warranted a prompt official investigation. Gustavo Zárate's allegations of ill-treatment are supported by the failure of the police to provide a warrant for his arrest and of the authorities to promptly inform his family of his place of detention, and by the use of incommunicado detention, allegedly for the purpose of obtaining a confession, which is prohibited by Article 20(ii) of the Constitution. The Amnesty International delegates were also struck by a number of statements attributed to the prisoner in the police reports which appeared quite implausible and strongly suggested that they were obtained under duress. Despite these disturbing elements of the case, the state government officials did not recognize any responsibility to investigate the complaint, and suggested that in many such cases complaints are made deliberately and deceitfully to evade prosecution.

Victórico Hernández Martínez and **Agustín de la Torre Hernández**
Amnesty International has adopted as prisoners of conscience two peasant leaders currently imprisoned in Chiapas, Victórico Hernández Martínez and Agustín de la Torre. Both are natives of Venustiano Carranza and members of the OCEZ, which is a constituent organization of the independent peasant coalition, the *Coordinadora Nacional Plan de Ayala* (CNPA), the Plan de Ayala National Coordinating body.

Victórico Hernández Martínez, well known locally as a leader of the *Casa del Pueblo*, a community organization in Venustiano Carranza, was arrested on 6 April 1981. He was charged with having participated in the murder of José Fonseca Hernández, a peasant killed on 26 June 1980, allegedly by a group of armed members of the *Casa del Pueblo*. Victórico Hernández Martínez was arrested together with Arturo Albores Velasco, a 31-year-old architecture student from Mexico City, who had been working on extension projects in the Venustiano Carranza area, sponsored by the *Universidad Nacional Autónoma de México* (UNAM), the National Autonomous University of Mexico. Agustín de la Torre Hernández was detained on the same charges on 24 February 1982. All three prisoners have consistently denied the accusations against them and have maintained that they were arrested as a result of official opposition to their legal political activities in their community.

Both Agustín de la Torre and Arturo Albores were said to have been ill-treated under police interrogation. Agustín de la Torre was held incommunicado in state judicial police premises in Tuxtla Gutiérrez for three days before being transferred to Cerro Hueco prison. His relatives told Amnesty International that he was bleeding profusely from the nose and mouth when they first visited him in prison. He was alleged to have been severely beaten and tortured with electric shocks and by having mineral water forced up his nose, in order to get him to sign a confession. Allegations of beating and ill-treatment were also made in the case of Arturo Albores Velasco, who was arrested on the same charge on 6 April 1981 and released on 2 December 1982 after the charge against him was dropped. He told Amnesty International that his eardrum was damaged as a result of being beaten after his arrest.

An appeal by the three prisoners in July 1982 for release on the basis of insufficient evidence for prosecution was rejected by the judge. They appealed against this ruling and the case went before the State High Court which in August 1982 ruled against them. On 22 November 1982 the state Attorney General dropped the legal proceedings against Arturo Albores Velasco, and he was released on 2 December 1982. In its written comments on his case, the Attorney General's office states that one of the considerations taken into account was that "the accused Arturo Albores Velasco was or is a young professional who ought to be given the chance to remake his life and be useful to society". Victórico Hernández Martínez and Agustín de la Torre Hernández were convicted by the court on 4 November 1983 on the murder charge and sentenced to 12 years' imprisonment. In the case of Victórico Hernández Martínez the trial took place more than two and a half years after the date of his arrest, although the maximum period stipulated by the Constitution is one year. There was an unsuccessful appeal against the verdict in January 1984. The two prisoners subsequently submitted an *amparo* appeal against their sentence to the Supreme Court of the Nation. A ruling by the Supreme Court, which could reduce or annul their sentence, was awaited at the time of writing (October 1985).

Both Victórico Hernández Martínez and Agustín de la Torre are known to have played a leading role as members of their organization and community in attempts to recover communal lands which they claim lawfully belong to their community. These attempts were made in the face of opposition from local landowners and businessmen, state and municipal authorities, and peasants aligned with the municipal authorities. Neither of the prisoners appears to have been involved in past acts of violence nor to have advocated violence to achieve their aims. Furthermore, there were a number of striking inconsistencies in the statements identifying José Fonseca Hernández' attackers made by the principal prosecution witnesses, all of whom belonged to a peasant faction in the village hostile to the *Casa del Pueblo*. Both prisoners have consistently maintained their innocence at all stages of the trial proceedings and since their conviction.

****

Amnesty International also adopted as a prisoner of conscience José Manuel Hernández Martínez, brother of Victórico, and also a community leader from Venustiano Carranza. He was arrested on 3 March 1984 and was being held at the time of Amnesty International's January 1985 mission in Venustiano Carranza prison on the same murder charge, and several other lesser charges. Amnesty International learned with satisfaction of his release on 23 February 1985, before his case had been brought to trial.

77

Photocopy of an official document signed by two local officials of the Public Ministry in Villa de las Rosas concerning the killing of peasant leader Elpidio Vázquez Vázquez on 9 September 1979. The document indicates that an official inquiry was opened into the killing (No. 18/979). In its reply to Amnesty International in January 1986 the government denied having any legal record of the case.

78

The town of Venustiano Carranza, in the rural Mexican state of Chiapas, viewed from above.

Tzotzil Indians outside the *Casa del Pueblo*, House of the People, Venustiano Carranza. The painted slogan reads: "This land has been paid for with our blood".

Protest march in Venustiano Carranza, Chiapas, August 1985. The banner bears the names of nine villagers killed on 6 October 1984 when their truck was ambushed by armed men.

José Rodríguez Mendoza, sugar-cane workers' leader, who was wounded on 27 July 1984 when the truck in which he was travelling was ambushed by armed men near the sugar mill of Pujiltic, Chiapas. A Guatemalan peasant, who was a passenger in the vehicle, was killed in the attack.

80

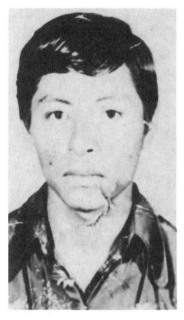

Victórico Hernández Martínez,
peasant leader from Venustiano
Carranza and member of the
*Organización Campesina Emiliano
Zapata* (OCEZ), the Emiliano
Zapata Peasant Organization. He
had played a leading role in attempts
to recover communal lands which he
claimed lawfully belonged to his
community. He was convicted of
having participated in the murder of
a peasant, on the basis of evidence
that Amnesty International regarded
as inadequate and inconsistent. He
was sentenced to 12 years' imprisonment and held in Cerro Hueco
prison, Tuxtla Gutiérrez. He was
adopted by Amnesty International as
a prisoner of conscience in July 1982.

Agustín de la Torre Hernández, a
member of the OCEZ, convicted on
the same charge as Victórico
Hernández Martínez, and also
sentenced to 12 years' imprisonment.
He was arrested on 24 February 1982
and held incommunicado in state
judicial police premises in Tuxtla
Gutiérrez for three days before being
transferred to Cerro Hueco prison.
His relatives told Amnesty International that he was bleeding
profusely from the nose and mouth
when they first visited him in prison.
He was alleged to have been beaten
and tortured with electric shocks and
by having mineral water forced up
his nose, in order to make him
sign a confession. He was adopted
by Amnesty International as a
prisoner of conscience in January
1984.

Andulio Gálvez Velásquez, lawyer and rural trade union leader, killed by gunmen on 4 October 1985 outside his office in Comitán. Andulio Gálvez was well-known locally for his legal work on behalf of peasants detained in connection with land disputes and for his assistance to peasant groups. He was also a candidate for the PSUM (Unified Socialist Party of Mexico) in the elections to the State Congress. He was one of several lawyers interviewed by Amnesty International during its March 1984 mission to Chiapas. His killing appeared to have been carefully planned — he was shot repeatedly outside his office in the centre of Comitán by four gunmen travelling in a car. His death followed an earlier unsuccessful attempt on his life and repeated death threats.

Gustavo Zárate Vargas, economics lecturer at the Autonomous University of Chiapas, detained in San Cristóbal de las Casas on 24 July 1983. He was released from prison on 1 March 1985, after a successful appeal to the Supreme Court against his conviction on drugs and arms charges. He alleged that he had been detained without a warrant and tortured for three days while held incommunicado. He stated that he was given electric shocks, beaten and threatened with execution if he did not sign a statement which he was not allowed to read. Amnesty International adopted him as a prisoner of conscience. It believed that statements he had made as a result of torture led to his conviction. No investigation was conducted into his allegations of torture.

A list of those killed and "disappeared" in Venustiano Carranza, Chiapas. The list is displayed in the building of the *Casa del Pueblo*, House of the People, a local community organization.

A shrine to murdered community leaders in Venustiano Carranza, Chiapas, in the *Casa del Pueblo*, House of the People.

The municipal prison, Venustiano Carranza, Chiapas.

84

Table 1

Reported killings in the San Juan Copala region, Oaxaca, between 1982 and 1985. See Chapter II for further information.

Name of victim	Date	Reported circumstances of killing[1]	Results of official investigations[2]
Regino de Jesús Flores	27 December 1982	Armed attack by civilians on villagers of Santa Cruz Río Venado. (Regino de Jesús Flores said to be MULT leaders.) At least two others wounded.	Criminal proceedings initiated against one person on murder charge. A warrant was issued for the arrest of two others, but the arrests were not carried out.
Feliciano Ramírez Merino	10 April 1983	Killed during fight with another villager, Pedro García López, a MULT member, in village of Rastrojo. According to press reports, the victim had been prompted by local officials to attack Pedro García, who had acted in self-defence.	The preliminary investigation, against Pedro García and five others, was concluded in April 1983. Legal proceedings were instituted against Pedro García. [In April 1985 he was sentenced to 20 years' imprisonment for murder.]3 Warrants for the arrest of the other five were requested by the Public Ministry.
Ramón Celestino Ramírez	24 July 1983	Killed in ambush near the village of Cruz Chiquita. Victim was a PRI official and village representative.	Three MULT members were arrested and charged with murder. The Public Ministry asked for warrants to be issued for the arrest of 21 others. [According to reports, the three detainees were acquitted and released in May 1984. All were members of the MULT.]

Amado González Flores Florencia Ramírez Salazar	27 October 1983	A MULT leader and his wife, they were killed in the hamlet of Cerro Cabeza. Culprits said to be officers of state preventive police stationed in Cruz Chiquita.	Criminal investigation opened but no result was reported. Amado González was wanted for arrest on a wounding charge.
Filemón Cruz Martínez	2 December 1983	A MULT leader, killed in his home in Cerro Viejo, reportedly by same police detachment as above accompanied by armed civilian.	A murder investigation was initiated, but no result was reported.
José Celestino de Jesús	17 November 1983	Said to have been wounded in an attack on his life in the village of La Ladera.	He was reported to have died during or as a result of the attack. A murder investigation completed on 18 January 1984, led to the issue of arrest warrants against 10 peasants, one of whom was detained in March 1984 and accused of murder. Another was arrested for wounding, but was released on 24 September 1984. [The peasant detained, Pedro Tomás Flores, is a MULT sympathizer.]
Tomás Santos Martínez	14 February 1984	No information.	Murder inquiry opened in Putla. Placed on file in absence of information on those responsible.
Domingo Nicolás Merino	25 February 1984	Killed in the village of Cerro Cabeza.	Murder inquiry opened 1 March 1984 against three people allegedly responsible, following denunciation to local authorities of San Juan Copala. No further statements obtained by Public Ministry and case placed on file on 11 September 1984.

| Victor Hernández Librado | 22 March 1984 | Victim was MULT leader from Rio Venado. His daughter, Tomasa Hernández Salas, also reported killed. | Murder inquiry completed and transmitted to judge on 27 March by Public Ministry of Putla. Warrants requested for the arrest of two people, but apparently no arrests made. There was no official record of the death of Tomasa Hernández Salas. |
| Julio Santillán | 25 March 1984 | A MULT sympathizer, killed in the village of Llano de Nopal. | Warrants issued for the arrest of nine people allegedly responsible. No arrests made. |

1 As documented in Amnesty International's October memorandum.

2 Summarized in information provided to Amnesty International mission delegates in January 1985 by the Attorney General of the state of Oaxaca.

3 Square brackets denote information received at a later date by Amnesty International.

Table 2

Reported killings in the Venustiano Carranza and Villa de las Rosas districts of Chiapas, between 1965 and 1985. See Chapter III for further information.

Name of victim	Date	Reported circumstances of killing	Result of official investigations
José Córdova Ayar	1966	The victim was an elected member of the *Comisariado de Bienes Comunales*, Commissariat of communal lands, of Venustiano Carranza. He was reportedly killed following his attempts to achieve legal demarcation of communal lands.	A criminal investigation was opened against one person on a wounding charge. He died 10 years later of natural causes. Apparently he was never arrested.
Manuel Gómez Ortega	1970	Also an elected member of the *Comisariado de Bienes Comunales* of Venustiano Carranza.	A criminal investigation was begun on 6 December 1970. Four people alleged responsible were remanded in custody but were acquitted by the court and released. There was an appeal against the verdict by the Public Ministry, and on 30 September 1971 the State High Court revoked the verdict of absolution, sentencing them to a nine-year prison term. The accused were never rearrested, however, and in July 1981 applied successfully to the judge to have the case closed.

Name	Date	Details
Bartolomé Martínez Villatorio Guadalupe Vásquez Gómez	1975	Bartolomé Martínez Villatorio was a member of the *Comisariado de Bienes Comunales* of Venustiano Carranza. There had been two previous attempts on his life. A criminal investigation into the murders failed to establish the identity of the culprits.
Miguel de la Cruz	October 1979	Member of CIOAC, reportedly killed when armed civilians attacked a political meeting in Villa de las Rosas, in which he was participating. No official information was available on this case. The Attorney General's office had no record of its having been reported.
Pedro Vásquez Vásquez	1979	No information. A criminal investigation was begun on 18 April 1979 against one person on a wounding charge. The victim gave a statement and a medical certificate was received. Legal proceedings were begun on 20 April 1970 and an arrest warrant was issued, but the person concerned was never apprehended.
Alfredo Morales Molina	1980	Member of CIOAC and peasant leader from Villa de las Rosas said to have been shot from a moving car during a political meeting. A preliminary investigation was begun on 30 June 1980. The body was identified and an autopsy carried out. There was no progress in establishing the identity of the culprits and on 4 July 1980 the case was placed on file.
Candido Velásquez Ruiz	October 1982	*Comisariado Ejidal* of the *Ejido* Flores Magón. A criminal investigation was begun on 16 October 1982. Depositions made by eye-witnesses led to the issue of a warrant for the arrest of one person, but he was never apprehended.

Response by the Mexican Government to Amnesty International's memorandum

Introduction

We refer to your letter of 22 November 1985, with which you kindly enclosed a copy of Amnesty International's report entitled: *Human rights in southeastern Mexico: Conclusions of an Amnesty International investigation into human rights violations in the states of Oaxaca and Chiapas.* The report presents the conclusions of a mission from your organization which visited Mexico between 26 January and 1 February 1985.

During that visit the Mexican authorities extended their assistance and support to resolve some queries which had arisen during an earlier mission by Amnesty International to the south of Mexico in March 1984.

In preparation for the visit, the Ministry of the Interior requested the cooperation of the relevant authorities, both at federal and state level, in helping to clarify certain events of concern to the Mexican Government and to Amnesty International. The state Governors of Chiapas and Oaxaca gave instructions to the Attorney Generals in their respective states for the necessary information to be collected, certain facts to be provided and precise details to be given on the progress of trials. In many cases, the information requested by Amnesty International made it necessary to pursue investigations going as far back as 18 years into the past, and to elucidate events on which that organization had only the most slender evidence. These efforts were made with the intention that the image and standing of Mexico and its state institutions should not be damaged by information which was not well-founded and which therefore presented a patently distorted view of the real situation prevailing in this country.

The Mexican authorities have a high esteem for the work of Amnesty International, and therefore feel it to be vital, in the interests of impartiality, objectivity and justice, which are its guiding principles, that Amnesty International should recognize that any judgment made about a particular situation should be founded on reliable evidence and not on partisan or one-sided assertions.

The Mexican Government understands that an institution of good faith which is apolitical and a defender of basic human rights, like

Amnesty International, must maintain an attitude of openness, allowing it to gather information on possible violations of individual rights and guarantees wherever they may occur. We presume that this same attitude should prevail at the stage when the organization is examining a report or piece of information. It is by proceeding in this way that a contribution can be made to the full restoration of human rights and their observance. If it were not so, one could expect a tendency towards bias and one-sidedness, inhibiting any possibility of a thorough clarification of matters of concern to the international community.

In the interviews held by members of Amnesty International with federal and state authorities in early 1985, the latter gave detailed answers to all the questions that were raised. It was expressly admitted that there are regrettable lapses in the administration of justice, which provide a constant incentive to reform and streamline procedures and methods of dealing with cases in dispute. Amnesty International's representatives were provided with the legal dossiers pertaining to the cases mentioned in the report, and the procedures of the Mexican legal system were fully explained to them. It should be remembered that at the time the Mexican authorities expressed concern that, notwithstanding the copious and impartial explanations they had been given in answer to their queries, the members of the mission remained sceptical. It would seem that this attitude, far from contributing to clarifying the cases with which we are concerned, can only help create insuperable obstacles to the investigation of the facts, and could even be interpreted as questioning the value of the information provided, for no other reason than its having been furnished by the government.

Regrettably, the fears that were expressed at that time have been borne out by the report to be published by Amnesty International. For this reason, and in order to give the facts the treatment they deserve, we formally request that this note, and the information about each case contained in the briefings appended to it, be added to your report. As will be evident, the Mexican Government remains willing to correct any misrepresentations that cast doubt on its traditional respect for the fundamental rights and liberties of mankind.

The Mexican Government wishes to reiterate that the statements in the report concerning the use of torture and cruel, inhuman and degrading treatment are, as the members of the mission were able to see for themselves, untrue generalizations. On the contrary, whenever the competent Mexican authorities have received reports of some abuse or arbitrary action, they have taken immediate steps to punish those responsible. To that end, during the legislative periods of 1983 and 1984 a number of reforms to the procedural and penal codes were put in hand. The members of the Amnesty International mission were given copies and full explanations of their provisions. Noteworthy among the changes is the elimination of the confession as an essential element of proof. It will only be sufficient evidence of guilt when it can be substantiated with other evidence. This avoids the possibility of a declaration obtained in dubious circumstances becoming an insurmountable obstacle for the accused person.

In addition, during its last period of sessions, the Senate of the Republic approved a bill on torture which will shortly be considered by the Chamber of Deputies. The bill embodies, in spirit, the concern expressed by the international community in the Convention Against Torture recently approved by the 39th General Assembly of the United Nations.

The suggestions regarding supposed complicity or concealment by the authorities in the commission of crimes affects the esteem in which the legal system and the democratic institutions of Mexico are held. As may be confirmed once again from the attached briefings, there is nothing that could serve as proof of such allegations. Proceedings have invariably been undertaken, as required by law, to investigate the facts of the case impartially, and to pursue, arrest and try the offenders.

With regard to the cases of "disappearances" mentioned in the report, it was considered imperative to provide information which would surely help remove confusion from a number of assertions which it contains. It is appropriate to point out that the Mexican Government has, for several years, collaborated with the Working Group on Enforced or Involuntary Disappearances, an organ of the United Nations Commission on Human Rights. Ample evidence of the role played by Mexico can be found in the annual reports submitted by the President of the Commission's Working Group.

On this point it is worth mentioning that, as has been said to the Working Group on many occasions, requests for information on alleged disappearances are often lacking in rigour. On numerous occasions complaints are dealt with that have not even been reported to the appropriate authorities. The result is that a variety of organiztions present long indiscriminate lists of people alleged to have "disappeared", about whom the Mexican Government has not even received due notification. The lists also include names which have been accepted in good faith by the international organizations and without any precise facts or basic information about the person, or the place and time of the supposed disappearance, activity, and so on. In these circumstances, the Mexican authorities have been obliged to undertake a difficult search which may take a long time or be unsuccessful.

The Mexican nation and its authorities at federal, state and municipal level have assumed full responsibility for the process of political, economic, social and cultural development which the country needs. The pursuit and administration of justice are based on the present constitutional charter. This document provides the foundation for the laws and regulations which govern our society. We Mexicans possess, in this basic legal framework, suitable instruments for the preservation of our fundamental rights. The *amparo* procedure constitutes an essential mechanism in the Mexican legal system, assuring the protection of our individual guarantees.

The history of our country reveals a deep-rooted tradition of law and respect for human rights. Consequently, one can discern in the spirit of our laws the contrasting realities of a developing country. The unfortunate inequalities that still affect Mexico mean that a system of defence counsel provided by the state is indispensable. Moreover, it has not escaped the notice of the competent authorities that the administration of justice must be made swifter and that undeniable deficiencies must be rectified.

We hope that Amnesty International will have due regard for the points raised above which amply confirm the political will of the government to achieve aims that are constructive and far-reaching in their social implications. Hence the request to give appropriate publicity to the points raised in this note and to the information in the briefings appended to it.

State of Oaxaca

Cases:

Luis Flores García

According to Amnesty International:

Luis Flores García, a Triqui Indian who had led community efforts to reclaim communal lands and had taken part in attempts to establish a producers' cooperative, was murdered in the hamlet of Paraje Pérez, allegedly by a group of civilians who were said to have been hired by local landowners. Quoting information provided by the Attorney General of the state, Amnesty International states that as a result of the investigations, four civilians were charged, one of whom was never arrested and the other three were detained and later sentenced to 30 years' imprisonment for assault and murder. In January 1979, however, the three appealed against the sentences, as a result of which they were released.

Our inquiries show that:

The information received by Amnesty International from the Attorney General of the state of Oaxaca regarding the murder of Luis Flores García is correct. On 12 August 1977, the preliminary investigation into the case was initiated. Ramón Celestino Ramírez, the alleged culprit, was turned over to the competent court, and arrest warrants were applied for in respect of the other accused parties.

Pablo Ramírez Flores and Martín Martínez were arrested on different dates.

At the end of the trial, the judge sentenced each of the three above-mentioned people to 30 years' imprisonment.

The defendants dissented from the verdict and appealed against it to the High Court of Justice of the state of Oaxaca. In view of the retraction of evidence by some witnesses and the non-appearance of others, the evidence on which the judge had based his sentence was found to be unsubstantiated and as a result the judgment was overturned.

It should be noted that the proceedings were conducted in strict accordance with the law. It is the right of any person who has been sentenced to ask for a review of the legality of the proceedings and the evidence adduced, such a review to be conducted by a different court to the one that tried the case.

Marcos Ramírez López

According to Amnesty International:
Marcos Ramírez López was allegedly murdered on 29 February 1980 in Concepción Carrizal (San Juan Copala). An investigation should be conducted into statements made by people said to be witnesses to the incidents.

According to the testimony of Roberto García López, Marcos Martínez López and he had gone to Culiacán, Sinaloa, to work as day-labourers, after detention orders had been served on them in San Juan Copala. In that city, together with Marcos Ramírez López, he was forcibly detained by state police, accompanied by a group of armed civilians from San Juan Copala. García López and Ramírez López were beaten and taken by the police to a prison and handed over to the civilians, who took them to Concepción Carrizal, near San Juan Copala.

Early on the morning of 29 February, now in Concepción Carrizal, Marcos Ramírez López was taken out of the room where he was being held, and shot. Roberto García López said that, still handcuffed, he managed to escape from his captors, who had been drinking heavily.

Quoting information provided by the state Attorney General, Amnesty International states that the victim's mother reported to the Agent of the Public Ministry that her son had disappeared on 5 June 1983. She said he had left for the fields and that, in her opinion, he had fled to escape arrest, there having been a detention order issued against him.

The organization says that the case was raised again with the state Attorney General in March 1985, when copies were sent of the statement of Roberto García Lopez and a report drawn up by a village leader and a group of neighbours (addressed to Oscar Flores Sánchez, then Attorney General of the Republic) which provides similar testimony with regard to the circumstances of the killing. However, Amnesty International says it is not satisfied that the allegations in the testimonies have been adequately investigated.

It is clear from our inquiries that:
The competent authorities were not informed through the legal channels available in Mexico (submission of a formal accusation to the appropriate Agent of the Public Ministry) that Marcos Ramírez López was allegedly killed in Concepción Carrizal (San Juan Copala, Oaxaca), after being abducted in Culiacán, Sinaloa.

Amnesty International mentions in its report that some documents were submitted "to Lic. Oscar Flores Sánchez, then Federal Attorney

General by a village leader and a group of neighbours". This is not a correct procedure to initiate any preliminary investigation, nor is the above-mentioned official competent to deal with the matter in question. Nevertheless, in view of your organization's request to the state Attorney General, serious inquiries were made into the incidents. These have as yet yielded no positive results despite the good intentions of the authorities in this state.

Juan Martínez López

According to Amnesty International:

Juan Martínez López was a leader of the MULT in the village of Yozoyuxi and disappeared after being detained by a group of civilians as he got off a bus in the hamlet of Concepción Carrizal near Yozoyuxi. Martínez López was returning from Mexico City where he had been negotiating on behalf of his organization with officials of the Ministry of the Interior.

On 2 December 1981 Carlos Fernández del Real sent a letter to the then Minister of the Interior, Professor Enrique Olivares Santana, in which he made a formal complaint and named four men said to be responsible for the abduction and disappearance of Juan Martínez López. In this letter he referred to the written denunciation which Triqui representatives had submitted to the Governor of Oaxaca in November 1981, in connection with the disappearance of Martínez López. Carlos Fernández del Real also mentioned an eye-witness who did not wish to be named and who claimed to have seen four individuals killing Juan Martínez López with their machetes.

In January 1985, a copy of this letter was sent by Amnesty International to the state Attorney General, requesting information on the current stage of investigations into the case of Martínez López. According to Amnesty International, however, no reply was received and there was no indication of any investigation having been opened.

Our inquiries show that:

This case displays similarities with the preceding one in that, despite the allusions to the disappearance and death of Juan Martínez López, no formal denunciation was made to the Public Ministry to enable the appropriate preliminary investigations to be set in motion.

Amnesty International points out that "a formal complaint was sent by a lawyer, Carlos Fernández del Real, to the then Minister of the Interior", although the Minister is not the right official to receive such notification, as the "lawyer" Fernández del Real, a legal expert, should have known, given the elementary nature of the matter to a person of his profession.

For this reason there has been no formal investigation whatsoever, from a legal point of view, on the specific question of the alleged arrest and murder mentioned above, since the procedure required to initiate the necessary legal steps (namely, that the Public Ministry should be informed of an alleged offence) has not been followed. Nonetheless, the state government, to show goodwill, has carried out inquiries in order to clarify this situation. So far it has had no success.

Camilo Martínez Cruz

According to Amnesty International:

Camilo Martínez Cruz was a MULT leader in the village of Santa Cruz Tilapa and was detained and killed in San Juan Copala by three individuals claiming to be members of the municipal police.

His mother, María Florencia Cruz, reported the killing to the state Attorney General, stating that her son's body showed signs of torture. In her statement, she identified eight individuals allegedly responsible for the murder of her son. Two other witnesses also testified against them.

Citing information provided by the state Attorney General Amnesty International indicated that an investigation had been opened, but pointed out that this had not resulted in any arrest.

Our inquiries show that:

In her initial statement before the Agent of the Public Ministry, María Florencia Cruz, mother of Camilo Martínez Cruz (or Juan Camilo Flores), stated that the incidents started after she and her son, now deceased, had been *imbibing intoxicating substances* and that she was unable to say when her son had left or which way he had gone.

She subsequently stated — she is presumed to have taken advice — that her son was taken away by eight men, who took the deceased "in the direction of the river", and that they were armed with machetes and knives. It should be mentioned that this last point is not at all conclusive, since it is frequent, in a rural area, for people to carry these implements which they use in their farm work.

As a result of her statement, arrest warrants were issued by the appropriate authority, which, on account of the legal and human problems involved, have not been carried out, despite the insistence of the state authorities.

Paulino Martínez Ramírez and María Francisca

According to Amnesty International:

On 21 February 1984, community leaders in Llano de Nopal made a formal complaint to the mayor of Juxtlahuaca concerning alleged abuses committed by a group of six individuals who apparently enjoyed the protection of the municipal authorities in San Juan Copala.

In one of their criminal acts, the assailants arrived at the home of Paulino Martínez Ramírez and his wife María Francisca. Paulino Martínez Ramírez was beaten, robbed and taken to prison; his wife was raped.

According to information provided by the state Attorney General, the police investigation into the case led to the issue of arrest warrants against the individuals who were named, at least one of whom was arrested.

Nevertheless Amnesty International reports the murder of María Francisca — although it has been unable to confirm this — as a reprisal by those who had committed the abuses.

Our inquiries show that:

Regarding the case of Paulino Martínez Ramírez and his wife, María Francisca, on completion of preliminary investigation No.116/984, Fernando Hernández Guzmán, Victoriano Hernández Martínez, Alberto Hernández Guzmán, and Alfonso Martínez Cruz were indicted on suspicion of having committed the crimes of breaking and entering, wounding, robbery and rape. They were remanded in custody and warrants were issued for the arrest of Francisco Pascual Martínez and Macario de Jesús. Those who were taken into custody are now undergoing trial.

As for the case of María Francisca, this person was indeed murdered, but not by the people guilty of the above-mentioned offences, nor was the murder in reprisal for having reported them to the authorities. The murderer was Paulino Martínez Ramírez, and the motive was one of passion, as is clear from the preliminary investigation, No.102/984, which explains how the murder was committed: with machete blows inflicted by Paulino Martínez Ramírez after a violent argument.

As a result, a warrant was issued for his arrest. He is currently a fugitive from justice.

Juan Albino
According to Amnesty International:

Juan Albino was a MULT sympathizer who was arrested with Julio Hernández López on 19 December 1983 in the village of La Ladera by police accompanied by armed civilians. According to witnesses' statements, Juan Albino and Julio Hernández López were tortured and taken to prison.

The bodies of Juan Albino and Juan Merino Bautista were found on 7 May 1984 after they had been secretly buried. The state Attorney General stated that investigations into the matter had been started, but that these had been closed in the absence of witnesses able to identify those responsible.

Our inquiries show that:

Regarding possible torture suffered by Juan Albino and a companion, no formal accusation has been submitted to any competent official, and it was thus not possible to carry out any preliminary investigation into the matter.

As for the subsequent murder of the same Juan Albino and Juan Merino Bautista, this was confirmed when the bodies were discovered buried in secret graves, but the culprits have yet to be identified and there have been no witnesses or other clues to suggest where the responsibility might lie. Furthermore, the person who reported the murder to the authorities, Camerino Andrés (brother of Juan Merino Bautista, despite the different surnames) disappeared and it has not been possible to discover his whereabouts.

Domingo Gonzáles Domínguez and Julio Sandoval Cruz
According to Amnesty International:

These people are MULT members in Yozoyuxi. In December 1984, they were both tortured and taken to state judicial police cells in the city of Oaxaca.

The case of Domingo González was denounced to the Governor of Oaxaca. Amnesty International sent a letter to the Attorney General of Oaxaca asking about the stage reached in the investigations, but so far has received no answer. The organization also states that Domingo González and Julio Sandoval have been accused of murder, the former on several counts.

Our inquiries show that:

The statement to the effect that Domingo González Domínguez (or Domingo González Guzmán) and Julio Sandoval Cruz are on trial for murder, is incorrect. The only case dossier in existence is No.25/984 on the basis of which legal proceedings are being taken against Domingo González Domínguez on a charge of wounding, the offended party being Pedro Celestino Ramírez.

In his preparatory statement before the trial judge, the accused never once declared himself to have been subjected to coercion or torture of any kind, nor are there in existence any medical certifications to confirm the use of methods such as these.

Paulino Martínez Delia
According to Amnesty International:

Paulino Martínez is a bilingual teacher and a MULT leader and was arrested on 24 April 1985 on several murder charges.

According to Paulino Martínez' account given to reporters, the police applied electricity and forced mineral water up his nose in order to make him confess to the murders. He was later made to sign blank documents.

On 27 April in the same year a doctor examined the prisoner and confirmed the existence of torture marks (a facsimile of the medical certificate was published in the weekly *Por Esto*).

In June the same year, Paulino Martínez was released after the charges against him were dropped. However, Amnesty International says that no official investigation has been carried out into the torture allegations.

Our inquiries show that:

Regarding the case of Paulino Martínez, the assertion that no official investigation has been carried out is not correct. This is evidenced by the existence of a preliminary investigation, No.65/85, against Doroteo Pacheco Santos, Pedro Hernández Hernández and Luis Pedro Aguilar Aragón, who are allegedly responsible for causing injuries to Paulino Martínez Delia. The dossier contains documents, medical certificates and official certificates attesting to the injuries inflicted.

The police officers responsible for causing these injuries were immediately relieved of their duties and, as already stated, brought to trial.

This shows that when there are complaints and evidence of practices which violate human rights, the authorities take steps to deal with the offences.

Gregorio Martínez Cruz, Tomás Alejandro Flores and José Guadalupe de Jesús

According to Amnesty International:

These people are local MULT leaders and were arrested in October 1983 and accused of killing a local PRI official.

The evidence against them was based on statements made by three of the victim's close relatives. The accused, in turn, denied the charges and brought witnesses to testify in their favour.

During the 1985 visit, Amnesty International was given the opportunity to examine the court records of this case. These showed, in the view of the Amnesty International delegates, that the evidence against the three accused was the statements of four witnesses, some of which were implausible or mutually contradictory.

The trial ended with the release of the prisoners. Tomás Alejandro Flores was released after a year in prison following the submission of an *amparo* appeal. Gregorio Martínez Cruz and José Guadalupe de Jesús were released after a year and a half in prison.

Our inquiries show that:

Gregorio Martínez Cruz, Tomás Alejandro Flores and José Guadalupe de Jesús were accused of the murder of Ramón Celestino Ramírez and duly brought to trial. It is true that, as Amnesty Inter-

100

national states, the trial went on for longer than is allowed by law. This was due to the practical difficulties posed by legal proceedings which were made necessary by the *amparo* petition filed by one of the defendants, appealing against the formal custody order; another delaying factor was the negligence of the defendants, as shown, for example, by the non-appearance of witnesses and the failure to appoint counsel for the defence when required.

Marcelino Guzmán Pérez
According to Amnesty International:
Marcelino Guzmán Pérez, a MULT leader in the village of Río Metate, was arrested on 13 October 1983, reportedly by municipal police from San Juan Copala accompanied by a group of armed civilians. He was accused of murder, together with six other people. Information provided by the state Attorney General included the testimonies of three witnesses for the prosecution.

In his preparatory declaration to the judge, Marcelino Guzmán declared his innocence and called a witness to testify in his favour. He also stated that he had been beaten and threatened with execution by the municipal police who arrested him.

According to information received by Amnesty International, Marcelino Guzmán was acquitted by the court and released on 27 February 1985, after spending almost a year and four months in prison. The Agent of the Public Ministry appealed against the verdict and the case was referred to the state High Court.

Our inquiries show that:
Trial proceedings were completed in full and concluded with the acquittal of Marcelino Guzmán Pérez. The verdict was appealed against by the Agent of the Public Ministry, who took his case to the state High Court of Justice, which upheld the acquittal verdict of the lower court.

Concerning the complaints of beatings suffered by the accused, although it is true that Marcelino Guzmán said that he had been beaten at the time of his arrest, this assertion was never satisfactorily proved, (although he did produce a certificate issued by a private doctor), nor did he make any official complaint against the people he believed to have been responsible.

Pedro Tomás Flores
According to Amnesty International:
Pedro Tomás Flores, an elderly Triqui Indian and a MULT sympathizer, was, like many other supporters of this organization, arrested without a warrant on charges of wounding and homicide. The charges were based on the testimony of people who had made practically identical statements in other trials.

Amnesty International took up his case after examining legal documents which suggested that the accused might have been the victim of a confusion of identities.

Our inquiries show that:
Amnesty International maintains that there have been a number of cases of unfair trials and concentrates its attention on the trial of Pedro Tomás Flores.
The Mexican Government is concerned that there should be no examples of any supposed errors such as can be said to have occurred in the case of this person. Nonetheless, the communication difficulties stemming from the person's ethno-cultural background are an obstacle to any prompt and conclusive explanation.

Juchitán

Torture and ill-treatment

Amnesty International has collected reports of alleged torture and ill-treatment inflicted on COCEI leaders and supporters. Some of these reports were published in the national press and others are documented in testimonies gathered by the organization's research delegation which visited Oaxaca.

From our point of view, however, although Amnesty International has received full and concise explanations concerning the incidents that took place in Juchitán, it has persisted in maintaining a biased view, reflecting opinions held by opposition tendencies who have transgressed the rule of law and whose members have had to be removed from power and imprisoned for inciting criminal offences.

Jesús Vicente Vázquez

According to Amnesty International:
Jesús Vicente Vázquez was arrested in December 1983 by plain-clothes police officers together with other COCEI leaders as he was on his way to an interview with an official of the Ministry of the Interior in Mexico City. Amnesty International states that, according to his statement, Jesús Vicente Vázquez and his companions were taken to a secret place of detention, where they were held incommunicado for seven days and were severely beaten while they were interrogated. They were later taken to a prison in Tehuantepec (Oaxaca). Altogether, Jesús Vicente Vázquez was held incommunicado for 12 days before a formal custody order was issued. Despite these irregularities, Amnesty International asserts that there was no indication in the official information on the case that any investigation had been conducted into the circumstances of his detention or into his complaints of ill-treatment.

Our inquiries show that:

The only source of the data collected by Amnesty International is the defendant, whose accusations are unverifiable, and they have ignored the information provided by the Mexican authorities, who have repeatedly asserted his guilt.

Jesús Vicente Vázquez was detained on 21 December and a formal custody order was issued on the 25th of the same month. There was thus no infringement of the General Constitution of the Republic. The trials of Jesús Vicente Vázquez have been conducted in strict conformity with the law and an appeal has now been lodged against the sentence of 10 years and six months' imprisonment handed down by the judge. The appeal is being heard in the High Court of Justice of the state of Oaxaca.

Rosalino Vázquez López, Miguel Guerra Vázquez and José Cruz Jiménez

According to Amnesty International:

These people were arrested on 1 January 1984 by the Juchitán municipal police and taken to the city hall where they were reportedly held incommunicado for eight days. During this time they were severely beaten, denied medical attention and continuously interrogated.

The information on these cases provided by the state Attorney General of Oaxaca shows that they were commited for trial on 7 January 1984 on various charges allegedly committed during disturbances which occurred on 1 January. On 2 June the same year they were released, after the court had granted an *amparo* petition. This shows that the municipal authorities illegally prolonged the preventive custody to which the defendants were subjected.

Our inquiries show that:

Amnesty International has acquired a biased view, having reached their conclusions on the basis of data obtained exclusively from defendants and opposition groups. There is no legal record whatsoever of the alleged ill-treatment or torture mentioned in the memorandum. For the rest, it is worth pointing out that Mexican justice, with the independence of judgment it provides in each legal action, decided to revoke, through the *amparo* procedure, the formal custody order which had been issued against them.

David Cruz Velázquez and Hermila Guerra López

According to Amnesty International:

These people, both COCEI supporters, were arrested on 1 January 1984 — reportedly without a legal warrant — by an officer of the state preventive police when they were visiting a sick friend in the hospital in Juchitán after the disturbances. They were later taken to a police station where they were held incommunicado and tortured. On 4 January they were moved to the municipal prison in Juchitán and on 11 January the court of first instance ordered their release for lack of evidence.

Amnesty International believes that these cases are only examples of the arrests carried out without lawful authority or reasonable cause, and of the torture and ill-treatment suffered by people suspected of being members of the COCEI.

Our inquiries show that:

The reply is as given for the cases of Rosalino Vázquez López, Miguel Guerra Vázquez and José Cruz Jiménez.

Political killings and disappearances

The Amnesty International report states, without naming its sources, that since 1974, when the COCEI was formed, more than 20 of its members have been killed, as a result, it would appear, of intense local opposition to their political principles. Although it admits that it does not have details of any previous alleged murders of COCEI members, it notes that the information on recent incidents suggests that, in a majority of cases, those responsible have not been brought to justice by the authorities.

The Mexican Government is concerned about the view taken by Amnesty International that people responsible for criminal offences committed in the country are not being pursued.

Víctor Pineda Henestrosa

According to Amnesty International:

Víctor Pineda Henestrosa, a primary school teacher, land reform official and COCEI member was seized, according to statements by his wife and three other witnesses (signed in the presence of the Agent of the Public Ministry in Juchitán), near the Juchitán bus station by six armed men (four of them wearing military uniform). His presumed abduction appeared to have occurred shortly before the elections for the post of commissioner for communal lands.

Amnesty International stated that the case was denounced on many occasions to the federal government and the military authorities but no reply was received.

Our inquiries show that:

It is intended to continue the investigation into the alleged disappearance of Víctor Pineda Henestrosa, and the Mexican Government will be grateful to Amnesty International for any reliable information which may help the authorities to discover his whereabouts.

Imprisonment

Jesús Vicente Vázquez, Leopoldo de Gyves Pineda, Carlos Sánchez López and Manuel Vázquez Nicolás

Amnesty International was concerned about the prolonged imprisonment of these people, arrested in December 1983 and who were still awaiting trial in prison in Tehuantepec (Oaxaca) as of January 1985. They were all COCEI members or were officials in the COCEI municipal government in Juchitán from 1981 to 1983. It is a matter of concern to Amnesty International that the criminal charges that have been brought against them appear to be based on inconsistent or unconvincing evidence and that they may have been imprisoned because of their non-violent activities as COCEI members and as Juchitán local government officials.

Our inquiries show that:

The legal processes of the Mexican Government, whether at federal, state or municipal level, would lose robustness, credibility and legitimacy, were they to give validity to unsound evidence. It would be an error of similar magnitude if government institutions were not to abide by the law when criminal acts were being committed. Regarding the cases of Carlos Sánchez López, Leopoldo de Gyves Pineda and Manuel Vázquez Nicolás, these people were brought to trial and finally set free on 16 August 1985.

State of Chiapas

Cases:

Elpidio Vázquez Vázquez

According to Amnesty International:

This person was a member of the *Central Independiente de Obreros Agrícolas y Campesinos* (CIOAC), the Independent Union of Agricultural Workers and Peasants, and was murdered by an unknown person at 11pm on 9 September 1979 in the centre of Villa de las Rosas. According to the testimony of Eliezer Grajales, the assailants arrived at Elpidio Vázquez Vázquez' house in a truck belonging to the municipality and opened fire on them. Rodríguez Ordoñez Santiago and Librado Arguello were taken into custody for their part in the incident, being released shortly afterwards. Nobody is thought to have been brought to trial for the killing.

Our inquiries show that:

José Rodríguez Mendoza, whose case history will be discussed below, was, at that time, leader of the CIOAC and, by means of this organization and through Maclovio Santís, had established a degree of control over the region, and particularly that municipality, which was hindering the work of the local, state and federal authorities, who were thus prevented from carrying out their statutory duties. As a result, when violent or bloody incidents occurred, they removed their own dead and wounded without reporting the crimes to the Public Ministry as required by law. The incident with which we are concerned was occasioned by differences stemming from the political and electoral contests in progress at the time. For the reasons given above, there is no record of the killing, no suspects were identified, no preliminary investigation was put in hand, nor were Rodrigo Ordoñez Santiago, then the elected mayor of Villa de las Rosas, or Librado Arguello arrested at any time.

The union and its influence have waned; there are no land-ownership disputes in the region, since by presidential resolution passed on 21 July 1937, 3,169-70-00 hectares were ceded to the peasants in the area, the resolution being implemented in full by Jorge Martín Ramírez Corona on 10 September 1938.

106

Tzaclum (Tzacacum), Municipality of Chalchihuitán

According to Amnesty International:

This place, located in the Central Highlands of Chiapas, was attacked by a group of armed civilians on 24 March 1983, resulting in the death of 11 people, mainly peasants, and a number of children. Many others stated that they had been wounded while trying to escape and that their homes had been burned down. The incident is attributed by Amnesty International, on the basis of press reports, to land-related conflicts between the local inhabitants and landowners who were ill-treating and systematically evicting them unless they agreed to make weekly payments; and the attack was carried out against the local inhabitants in reprisal for their efforts to separate from the municipality.

As a result of investigations carried out by the authorities, 15 people were detained, including Nicolás López Gómez, who was mayor at the time, and local officials. Others evaded arrest and nobody else was formally accused of the killings. Amnesty International further states that during the delegates' visit in 1984 reports were received of fresh attacks in the region on sympathizers of the Independent Union of Agricultural Workers and Peasants (CIOAC) and the "Emiliano Zapata" Peasant Organization (OCEZ), carried out by armed civilians or gunmen presumed to be members of the *Confederación Nacional Campesina* (CNC), National Peasant Confederation.

Our inquiries show that:

The following facts, *inter alia*, are documented in testimonies in the possession of the state Attorney General's office: on 25 March 1983, the state judicial police filed a report with the Public Ministry that in the place known as Tzaclum (Tzacacum), in the municipality of Chalchihuitán, which falls within the judicial district of Simojovel, a violent clash had occurred resulting in deaths and injuries. An investigation, No.897/2°/983, was carried out and a visit was made to the scene of the incidents to record what had happened.

On arriving at the scene of the incidents, the investigators from the Public Ministry found a number of huts which had been torn apart and set alight. They also found the charred corpses of the following people; Nazaria Díaz López, upper and lower limbs consumed by fire; Manuel López Díaz, with the head facing westwards and the limbs in the opposite direction; María Pérez López, upper and lower limbs totally consumed by fire; María López Pérez, a minor, burnt; Manuel López Girón, burnt in the fire; Martín López Díaz, slightly burnt, and showing dislocation of the right elbow produced by a gunshot, and other bullet wounds to the body; Domingo Núñez López and Bartolo Núñez Díaz; Augustín Pérez Díaz, showing multiple lacerations; Sebastián Núñez López, showing four gunshot wounds; Mariano Núñez López, showing multiple lacerations and total severance of the head. The 11 corpses were properly identified in due course.

Eight testimonies, all consistent with one another, establish that: at 4am on 24 March 1983, the village of Tazclum, in the municipality of Chalchihuitán, was attacked by 20 men armed with rifles, machetes and burning torches, who fired on (the inhabitants) and set fire to all their huts, killing all those who were unable to escape. The attack is attributed to the fact that the inhabitants were unwilling to give between 100 and 200 pesos to the religious authorities in Chalchihuitán, who were making demands every other day for payment for the St Paul's Day festivities, giving the attackers reason to think they had abandoned the Catholic faith. It was made clear that *the attack was in no way politically motivated*, since the assailants do not belong to any political party.

Another 15 testimonies, all mutually consistent, show clearly that: one of the assailants, Salvador Girón Díaz, a religious leader and the local mayor, as well as Nicolás López Gómez, Agustín Gómez López and Mario Gómez Girón, organized a meeting of the townspeople, which was attended by some 800 people from different villages, who were told that Tzaclum did not want to contribute to the St Paul's Day celebrations, that they did not belong to the Catholic church anymore, and did not respect God. Having stirred up the crowd with these arguments, the local chiefs distributed bottles of petrol and ordered them to kill (the inhabitants of Tzaclum) and set fire to their huts. They also gave them each a white cloth to wear on their heads to show who they were and brandy to give them courage. Salvador Girón Díaz took one of the four rifles and three pistols which were used in the attack and fired it into the air in view of the crowd to show that they really worked.

On 13 April the following were turned over to the Attorney General's office, accused of criminal offences: Nicolás López Gómez, Domingo Gómez López, Salvador López Núñez, Mariano García Pérez, Nicolás Pérez Gómez, Nicolás Gómez Girón, Agustín Rodríguez Domínguez, Martín Pérez Díaz, Lorenzo Girón Pérez, Manuel Rodríguez Sánchez, Cándido Díaz Pérez, Mariano Díaz Girón, Enrique López Gómez, Vicente García Gómez, Mariano Gómez Gómez and Martín García Girón. Statements were taken from them and they admitted responsibility for the crimes of which they were accused.

The factual statements, all of which are consistent with one another, affirm that on the day of the events in question representatives from several local communities gathered in the main square of Chalchihuitán. The names of 40 of them were given in full and are listed in

108

Annex 1 attached. The statements are agreed in saying that the orga-
nizers were Domingo Sánchez Pérez, Nicolás Sánchez Pérez, Salvador
López Núñez, Nicolás López Gómez and Salvador Girón Díaz, and
that they were responsible for organizing a gathering on 13 March
1983 of the people from surrounding communities and telling them
what they were going to do; the arrangement was that they would
meet again on 23 March to carry out their plan. At both meetings they
told them not to be afraid and that the Tzaclum people had not paid
their religious dues. The statements also say that Salvador Girón Díaz
was the main instigator and that on the day of the incidents he gave
the signal to attack the village by exploding a Molotov cocktail.

On 14 April 1983 preliminary investigations were instituted, initial
statements were taken, and on 27 April 1983 custody orders and
arrest warrants were issued for conspiracy with criminal intent,
wounding, first degree murder and causing damage to property,
against the 25 people involved, whose names are listed in Annex 5.
They included Salvador Girón Díaz, the main instigator, religious
leader and mayor of Chalchihuitán. The accused appealed for *amparo*
but this was denied by the state district judge. On 15 October the pre-
siding judge pronounced the case beyond his competence and the
writs were passed to the judge of first instance, responsible for both
civil and criminal cases in Simojovel, the legal district in which the
incidents occurred.

From the High Court of Justice we obtained the following information: in the appeal judgment, it appears that the district judge of
first instance for Simojovel, Chiapas, passed definitive sentence in
penal dossier No.133/984 against the 21 people involved in the incidents, who are listed in Annex 6, for wounding, homicide and causing
damage to property. The judgment went through the normal process
of appeal and was upheld by the criminal branch of the High Court.
The following considerations were cited: the evidence was fully substantiated, the confessions given to the Public Ministry and the judge
were validated in their entirety; the 14 retractions made before the
trial judge were dismissed on the basis of jurisprudential arguments
and of lack of supporting evidence. The charge of homicide during
an affray was also not accepted since this requires that there should
be no prior agreement and in this case there were two preparatory
meetings, on 13 and 23 March 1983. The court of appeal corrected
the ommission of the lower court in not imposing individual sentences,
each of the guilty people being sentenced to 21 years in prison, 20
years for first degree murder, six months for wounding and six
months for damage to property. All the sentenced people are now in
Cerro Hueco prison in Tuxtla Gutiérrez, Chiapas.

Comments

All those involved in the incidents are indigenous Tzotzils with very little education and, as peasants, living in precarious economic conditions. They are easy prey to religious fanaticism, and although in theory they are of the Catholic faith, they bring to their worship strong pagan influences originating in their ancestral culture and mystical traditions. The social fabric is totally conditioned by this culture. In this case, the religious authorities are also spiritual fathers and leaders of indigenous congregations. Owing to the sway they hold over the local communities and the total submission shown towards them by the inhabitants, they are frequently chosen as municipal officials.

In Tzaclum, Chalchihuitán, the inhabitants, as their own confessions and the experience of state officials confirm, have never belonged to the Independent Union of Agricultural Workers and Peasants (CIOAC) or to the "Emiliano Zapata" Peasant Organization (OCEZ), nor are the authorities aware of any other attack similar to the one under consideration having occurred. There are no agrarian disputes in the region, since the village of Chalchihuitán and its dependency Tzaclum were, by presidential resolution dated 26 March 1975 and published in the *Federal Daily Gazette* of 29 August 1975, granted an area of 17,948-24-16 hectares, the resolution being fully implemented on 19 October 1981 by Wilber Durán Avila.

Nevertheless, it should be noted that: of the 20 people who were detained at the start of the criminal investigations, 18 were individually sentenced to 21 years in prison (Annexes 4 and 6). Of these, only two were religious leaders, instigators and attackers (Annexes 3 and 6). Although warrants were issued for the arrest of Salvador Girón Díaz, religious leader, Mayor of Chalchihuitán and the most prominent instigator of the attack, and of the ring-leaders, Salvador Girón Díaz was not arrested.

Andrés Domínguez Rodríguez and José Rodríguez Mendoza
According to Amnesty International:

José Rodríguez Mendoza, caneworkers' leader and a leading member of the *Unión de Ejidos 28 de Septiembre*, 28 September Union of *Ejidos*, was ambushed in his van by gunmen near the "El Coyol" ranch, with the result that his passenger, Andrés Domínguez Rodríguez, was shot dead and Rodríguez Mendoza was badly wounded. At the time the Amnesty International memorandum was prepared the culprits had not been identified.

Our inquiries show that:

The incidents referred to by Amnesty International occurred at 1.30pm on 27 June 1984 on a dirt road to the "Agua Bendita" ranch, at a place known as "Las Trancas". Here José Rodríguez Mendoza and Andrés Domínguez Ramírez were ambushed, resulting in the wounding of the former and the death of the latter. Rodríguez Mendoza showed seven bullet wounds in the left forearm and his passenger had a single wound in the right parietal, shattering the skull. No assailants or suspects have been identified to date.

The conclusion reached in respect of these incidents is that the wound Rodríguez Mendoza suffered was self-inflicted and that he also murdered his passenger in order to be able to leave the state with honour. The evidence for this is as follows:

1. As he was driving, the bullets could only have struck him in the shoulder, head or face;
2. If Rodríguez Mendoza had lost consciousness, and the aim of the attackers was to kill him, they would have had ample time to do so;
3. The paraffin wax test on both men's right hands was positive, despite Rodríguez Mendoza's claim not to have used a firearm in 10 years;
4. The marks left by the shots showed them to have been fired from a distance of 80cm., which would have enabled Rodríguez Mendoza easily to identify his assailants. He did not do so;
5. The position of the corpse showed the deceased to have had his hands raised, which would not be the case in the event of a surprise attack;
6. The traces found at the scene of the incident were arranged in such a way as to suggest that they had been left deliberately.

There is no indication that the above incident was occasioned by land-related conflicts.

Domingo Calvo Espinoza and eight others
According to Amnesty International:

At 7pm on 6 October 1984, 17 peasants from the village of Venustiano Carranza belonging to the "Emiliano Zapata" Peasant Organization (OCEZ) were on their way to help companions of theirs whose vehicle had run out of petrol at the "El Roblar" ranch when they were attacked by some 100 peasants who, despite their victims being unarmed, fired on them indiscriminately, leaving nine dead, including a 12-year-old child, and four wounded. According to Amnesty International the assailants were members of the National Peasant Confederation (CNC) and belonged to a group called *Los Pariseños*. The motive for the attack appeared to be vengeance following the killing of their leader, Bartolo Gómez, for which *Los Pariseños* held the OCEZ responsible. Amnesty International was informed that 13 peasants from the CNC had been detained but that

12 of these had been released. The organization was also told that the 12 were brought to trial and sentenced to four years' imprisonment for homicide during an affray, but were later freed on bail. It points out that the penal code then in force prescribed a penalty of 10 to 20 years for first degree murder, but that the sentenced prisoners were released from custody due to what was regarded by the authorities as the impossible task of assessing individual responsibility.

Our investigation shows that:

This conflict stems from the compensation granted for flood damage to land caused by the construction of the "La Angostura" dam and reservoir. This issue brought about a division between the peasants of "La Casa del Pueblo" who are members of an indigenous community and live in the village of Venustiano Carranza, and whose organization was dominated by the *Coordinadora Nacional "Plan de Ayala"* (CNPA), Plan de Ayala National Coordinating body, and by peasants belonging to the "Paraíso de Grijalva" group, who are members of the CNC.

The peasants belonging to "Paraíso de Grijalva" owned most of the land submerged by the reservoir. The compensation money of seven million pesos was, however, given to the Commission of Communal Lands in Venustiano Carranza, that is, to thé "Casa del Pueblo", who were unwilling to share it out. In addition to the money, they were given a thousand head of cattle, tractors and other goods, which they dealt with in the same way. This one factor led to a conflict within the "Casa del Pueblo" and led to the departure from it of the original members of the community (*comuneros básicos*).

The original members, or "coras", allied themselves with those belonging to the "Paraíso de Grijalva" and abandoned those who were still members of the "Casa del Pueblo". These, in order to strengthen their weak position, affiliated to the CNPA and the OCEZ. The original community members made a formal complaint against the "Casa del Pueblo" members, following which a visual inspection of the tractors, trucks and cattle was ordered. The cattle were being kept on four ranches: Majatic, El Roblaje, Egtalco and Altos de Jalisco. Most of these livestock areas are located in the area controlled by the "Paraíso de Grijalva" members, so that the "Casa del Pueblo" members would be obliged to pass through their land. To avoid the inspection the "Casa del Pueblo" members decided to transfer the herd from Los Altos de Jalisco to El Roblaje, and in so doing destroyed pens and wire fencing belonging to *Los Pariseños*, who were very upset and indignant as a result.

While this task was being undertaken, one of the "Casa del Pueblo" vehicles ran out of petrol and some of the members headed for the local town to get more, while those now deceased stayed behind to guard the vehicle. At that moment the "Paraíso de Grijalva" people came by. They were full of resentment at the killing, nine days earlier, of Bartolo Gómez Espinoza, the leader of their allies, the original community members, and were on their way from the cemetery at the end of the period of mourning. When the two groups came face to face the driver of the "Casa del Pueblo" vehicle attacked and punched Bartolo Gómez Morales and they threw stones at his companions, and then ran away. *Los Pariseños* went back to their village, gathered their friends together and handed out weapons, and returned to where the truck had run out of petrol to wait for the "Casa del Pueblo" people. When they arrived, the attack occurred.

The agrarian dispute in the area has its origin in the concession on 20 July 1965 of an area of 50,152-95-42 hectares to the members of the community, by a presidential resolution which was implemented on 10 November 1974 by Elios Muñoz López. Only 46,968-40-00 hectares were actually handed over; the reason for the shortfall of 3,184-55-22 hectares was quite simply that these hectares did not exist, the error making it impossible to execute the resolution. In spite of this, and the arguments deployed to convince the members of the community of this fact, they have persisted with their claims. The legal fund of the village of Venustiano Carranza is included in the presidential resolution for the members of the community and of the 5,000 hectares in existence, they claim 2,500 for themselves. This has fostered an attitude of non-acceptance among the resident population, and even the mayor has expressed his opposition to the demands. In this way the divisions between the two sides have been deepened.

From the appeal verdict 337/A/985 registered in the High Court of Justice it can be seen that:

An appeal was brought against the sentence of first instance passed on 10 May 1985 condemning Bartolomé Velázquez and Bartolo Gómez to four years each in prison for homicide committed in the course of a quarrel, and one year in prison for wounding the people listed in Annex 1. The facts contained in the appeal dossier are in general agreement with what is set out above, but according to the statements of the four injured parties, the incidents were as follows: after one truck carrying 20 to 24 people had run out of petrol, they got into another three ton truck to be taken to their destination. Before they arrived at "El Roblar", 30 men suddenly emerged from the woods and began to shoot at them. The sentenced men, Bartolomé Vázquez Velázquez and Bartolo Gómez stated that they were attacked by the "Casa del Pueblo" people and returned their fire with the weapons they were carrying. The appeal court considered that both the "Casa del Pueblo" people and the "Paraíso de

Grijalva" people were equally responsible for the clash in which they had participated in order to settle their differences, which stemmed from political problems and problems concerning the ownership and tenure of land. The sentences were upheld and the rearrest of the two sentenced people was ordered.

It should be pointed out that 11 people, whose names are given in Annex 3, were acquitted by the court of first instance.

Juan Gómez Cruz and Leandro García López

According to Amnesty International:

Juan Gómez Cruz, Municipal Agent of the village of Ostuacán and a member of the "Emiliano Zapata" Peasant Organization (OCEZ) was fatally shot in the neighbourhood of Lindavista on 22 December 1984. Amnesty International accuses cattlemen loyal to the National Peasant Confederation (CNC) of the murder, the motive being the refusal to allow them grazing rights on *ejidal* land. The organization also mentions that this same group attacked another OCEZ member, Librado García López, wounding him with machetes. Although the incident was denounced, Amnesty International states that the investigation has not led to any arrests.

Our inquiries show that:

This is mainly an agrarian conflict. The initial extension action in the municipality of Ostuacán or, to be precise, in the village of Lindavista (Plan de Ayala) stems from the application submitted on 18 May 1956. The order from the state Governor was issued on 26 February 1958 and was negative on the grounds of the ineligibility of the proposing group, and the dossier was therefore passed to the regional chamber of the agrarian consultative body by official letter No.10031 dated 1 October 1985.

Due to the lack of instruments regulating and guaranteeing land tenancy, and the atomization that land distribution is producing in the state, invasions of peasants against cattle ranchers and vice versa are very frequent, and may affect one hectare or an unlimited number. This killing occurred because the cattle ranchers invaded an area jointly owned by indigenous people, and the death followed a clash between two groups of about 40 ranchers and 30 indigenous people.

These events led to the opening of preliminary investigation No.389/984. Legal dossier No.23/985 shows the accused as being Salvador Gómez Izquierdo, Jesús Alvarez Morales and Eduardo Ramírez Sánchez, only the first of whom was actually detained, the others being fugitives from justice. The proceedings are at a stage where sentence will soon be passed.

Leandro García López, mentioned by Amnesty International as

114

having been injured the day after the death of Juan Gómez Cruz, is accused, jointly with Carlos Castro and Fernando García López, of the murder of Alberto Sánchez Lara, in incidents said to have occurred on 11 November 1985, also in the neighbourhood of Lindavista. The legal dossier is No.172/985. Although arrest warrants have been issued for the three men, no one has yet been taken into custody.

Enrique Vázquez Hernández and Alejandro Aguilar Pérez

According to Amnesty International:

Hostility between the Independent Union of Agricultural Workers and Peasants (CIOAC) and the National Peasant Confederation (CNC) over the use of *ejidal* land was the reason for an ambush on 27 January 1985 on Enrique Vázquez Hernández and Alejandro Aguilar Pérez, members of the regional committee of the CIOAC, who were returning from one of their political meetings. Vázquez Velázquez was struck by a bullet in the shoulder. A formal complaint was made to the Public Ministry naming six people, including three CNC members and one local landowner. No arrests appear to have been made. Amnesty International states that in the district of "Las Margaritas", CIOAC leaders have been the object of further attacks and killings and that in three of the incidents the same gunman has been identified.

Our inquiries show that:

This region is free from agrarian conflicts. By a presidential resolution of endowment dated 21 July 1933 in favour of the municipality of "Las Margaritas" or, to be precise, the village of the same name, 2,858-31-00 hectares were ceded to it, divided into the following portions: "Las Cruces" hacienda: 424-51-40 hectares; "San Sebastián" hacienda: 1,804-44-60 hectares; and "San Joaquín" hacienda: 629-35-00 hectares. This resolution was implemented in full on 11 April 1934 by Moisés Márquez Muñoz.

The case should be seen in the context of the two following ones, which are both closely linked with it. In this incident, the interests involved were not to do with land conflicts, but were the result of a struggle between individual interests and arguments about the distribution of profits from wood belonging to the *ejidos* of "Piedra de Huixtla", "Santa Rita" and "Justo Sierra", controlled by the redoubtable gunman Julio Pérez Pérez, described by Amnesty International as a hired gunman.

Vázquez Velázquez was on the side of Andulio Gálvez Velázquez, and was attacked for this reason by Julio Pérez Pérez, to whom the last attempt on his life in January 1985 is attributed. The investigations led to the arrest of two people, but Julio Pérez Pérez was not detained. He is now dead. The landowner mentioned in the report is

Ernesto Castellanos Domínguez, brother of the state Governor and a small landowner who has been a farmer for a long time and has been unjustly implicated in these events.

Gregorio López Aguilar
According to Amnesty International:
On 6 August 1985, this person was murdered. He was an official at the "Las Margaritas" *ejido* and a local leader of the Independent Union of Agricultural Workers and Peasants (CIOAC). In the same incident Hilario Jiménez López and Ajilio Trejo Jiménez were wounded. These incidents have been attributed to the Commissioner of a neighbouring *ejido*, a member of the National Peasant Confederation (CNC), who was charged with responsibility when the crime was denounced. According to Amnesty International, it was reported in the press that the attack was the result of personal conflicts and that the preliminary investigations showed that the alleged aggressor had acted in self-defence; responsibility for the attack was attributed to the same person who had attacked Enrique Vázquez Hernández and Alejandro Aguilar Pérez, and who, despite the issue of an arrest warrant in his name, had not yet been captured. Amnesty International further states that, according to the same sources, the root problem was a claim for 150 hectares under private ownership and the resulting conflicts that have arisen with the landowner, a close relative of the Governor.

Our inquiries show that:
Gregorio Pérez Aguilar, alias "El Galo", not Gregorio López Aguilar, as Amnesty International calls him, was killed by Julio Pérez Pérez, for reasons already explained, namely the profits of the wood whose control was being disputed by Andulio Gálvez Velázquez. A warrant was issued for the arrest of Julio Pérez Pérez for the murder of Gregorio Pérez Aguilar and for wounding Ajilio Trejo Jiménez and another person.

Andulio Gálvez Velázquez
According to Amnesty International:
Andulio Gálvez Velázquez was shot and killed at 7pm on 4 October 1985 by four gunmen travelling in a green Volkswagen. He was a PSUM (Unified Socialist Party of Mexico) candidate for local deputy, a lawyer and political education secretary in the state committee of the Independent Union of Agricultural Workers and Peasants (CIOAC). Gálvez Velázquez was well known for his defence of peasants arrested in connection with land ownership problems. The killing occurred in Comitán and was preceded by other acts of aggression, including an attack on his own home and on that of Enrique Vázquez Hernández. Amnesty International further states

that on the next day two employees of the Credit Union for which Andulio Gálvez Velázquez worked were detained and tortured in an attempt to make them confess to the crimes; and that two people arrested for the murder were members of the National Peasant Confederation (CNC).

Our inquiries show that:

Andulio Gálvez Velázquez, at the time of his death, was manager of a credit association of coffee growers named the *Union Nacional de Crédito Forestal y de Agroindustrias de Ejidatarios* (UNCA-FAESA), an institution which handles millions of pesos, and a leader of the CIOAC, operating in the regions of La Trinitaria and Comitán. To exercise his power more effectively, he allied himself with Margarito Ruíz Hernández, with whom he later became on less friendly terms after he left his family to become the lover of the woman who had previously been the mistress of Ruíz Hernández and whose name was Marisela Coello.

The large sums of money passing through the hands of these three people, attributed by some to possible fraud within UNCAFAESA, made them eager to extend their dealings and their influence to other sectors, and they planned and executed a murder attempt on Julio Pérez Pérez to remove from him control of the wood in the *ejidos* of "Piedra de Huixtla", "Santa Rita", "Sonora" and "Justo Sierra". An investigation was therefore undertaken into the charges of attempted murder, using a firearm and causing damage to property, perpetrated against Julio Pérez Pérez and others. The case is currently under investigation and no indictment has yet been made.

In due course a preliminary investigation, No.467/985, was opened, and later combined with investigation No.408/985, into the charge of first degree murder arising from the killing of Andulio Gálvez Velázquez, in the judicial district of Comitán, at 7pm on 4 October 1985. The accused, Feliciano García Pérez and Arturo Pérez Pérez, were turned over to the competent judicial authorities, having confessed, in the course of the investigation, to being implicated in the crime. In these proceedings it was also requested that warrants be issued by the trial court for the arrest of Julio Pérez Pérez and Alvaro "N".

The proceedings, which took place immediately after the death of Gálvez Velázquez, were conducted in the presence of the state Attorney General and the Director of Specialist Services of that department. Initial inquiries suggest that, at the very moment he was attacked, Andulio Gálvez Velázquez recognized Julio Pérez Pérez as one of his assailants; the latter was already the subject of an arrest warrant on charges of assault in a deserted place and carrying firearms, perpetrated, as it happened, against Gálvez Velázquez,

Margarito Ruiz Hernández and others.

Felipe de Jesús Santís and Eleazar Velazco, accountant and field inspector with UNCAFAESA, respectively, were witnesses to the murder. They were in the UNCAFAESA offices and on hearing the shots immediately went into the street, and found Gálvez Velázquez dead a few metres away. Their detention was solely for investigatory purposes and not to charge them with the murder.

Following the death of Gálvez Velázquez, 900 9mm M-1 cartridges, wrapped in blankets with "CIOAC — PSUM" and a hammer and sickle printed on them, were taken from a house in Comitán. These objects were on view at the state Attorney General's office.

Julio Pérez Pérez was arrested shortly afterwards. He escaped from prison and on 19 November 1985, at about 2pm in the area which encompasses "Santa Rita", "Sonora" and "Piedra Huixtla", in the municipality of "Las Margaritas", he was killed together with Francisco Hernández Pérez, which led to the opening of investigation No.549/985.

Gustavo Zárate Vargas

According to Amnesty International:

Gustavo Zárate Vargas, a 30-year-old professor of economics at the Autonomous University of Chiapas in San Cristóbal de las Casas, a member of the Workers' Revolutionary Party (PRT) and coordinator of the social sciences faculty, took part in campaigns for internal reforms in the university and for the reinstatement of a group of workers who had been dismissed from the *Instituto Nacional Indigenista*, National Institute for Indigenous Peoples. He also provided support to Guatemalan refugees. He was arrested by the state judicial police on 24 July 1983. Gustavo Zárate Vargas considered his arrest to have been illegal and on 4 August 1983 filed a petition for *amparo* against his custody order. He told the press that when he was arrested the judicial police showed no warrant for his arrest, that his house was searched, and that he was subjected to torture, being beaten on the head and body and having mineral water forced into his nostrils. When interviewed by Amnesty International in March 1984 in Cerro Hueco prison in Tuxtla Gutiérrez, he confirmed his previous statement, and added that he had had electricity applied to his nose, ears and genitals, had been beaten with a wet towel and had been forced to sign a statement which he was not allowed to read and was threatened with death if he failed to do so.

The documentation examined by Amnesty International shows Gustavo Zárate Vargas to have been accused of holding suspicious meetings in his home with foreigners, using his home to store arms, marijuana and drugs, and possessing pamphlets and books on political subjects. Amnesty International considered that Gustavo Zárate

Vargas had been imprisoned because of his non-violent political activities and adopted him as a prisoner of conscience.

The case was handed over to the Federal Public Ministry and on 5 December 1983 he was found guilty and sentenced to eight years' imprisonment, reduced on appeal to seven years and three months. On 23 November 1984 the Supreme Court of Justice found that there had been irregularities in the trial and the sentence was reduced to two years and three months. He was released on bail on 1 March 1985.

Our inquiries show that:

The facts are as follows: in the house located at No.35, Calle Yajalón, San Cristóbal de las Casas, noisy disturbances often occurred, guns were fired and, in addition, weapons were stored, and as a result of neighbours' complaints a preliminary investigation, No.2200 bis/1/83, dated 20 July 1983, was opened against Gustavo Zárate Vargas, supported by a report from the Chief of the state judicial police which attested to the truth of the complaint. The judge of first instance in the district was therefore asked to proceed to an inspection of the house and, when a search warrant had been obtained, the police asked the Public Ministry for assistance. The search resulted in the removal from Gustavo Zárate Vargas of certain objects found in the house, namely 75 .22 cartridges, 50 9mm. bullets, a .22 calibre pistol with chamber and eight live cartridges, three home-made bombs, two daggers and a packet containing marijuana. As a result the judicial police turned Gustavo Zárate Vargas over to the competent authorities, together with the confiscated objects.

In his statement, Gustavo Zárate Vargas declared that in the social science field there were two warring student groups, one led by teachers of Argentine nationality and the other formed by himself, who had had frequent confrontations and as a result of some of these he had himself been injured by gunshots. He also stated that he was a member of the *Partido Revolucionario de los Trabajadores* (PRT), Workers' Revolutionary Party, and that for self-defence he had manufactured some 30 explosive devices, admitting ownership of the three that had been found in his house and also of the firearm.

He went on to state that, in cooperation with the PRT, he provided protection and assistance to Guatemalan refugees, and that these were mainly guerrillas seeking refuge in the state. He also said that he imported large-bore weapons from Belize for the warring students and that the marijuana in his possession belonged to his friend Javier Quiñones who left it in his house after one of his meetings. On 25 July he confirmed his statement to the Public Ministry, admitting that he was guilty of the charges against him and that he owned the articles described above. He also admitted giving help to Guatemalan guerrillas, including protection and financial assistance, in full knowledge of the illegality of their presence on Mexican soil; he also declared that he was a full-time teacher at the University of Chiapas, with a salary of 47,000 pesos.

As this investigation was under federal jurisdiction, the state Attorney General's office declared the matter beyond its competence and passed the preliminary investigation, together with the confiscated objects to the Agent of the Federal Public Ministry in Tuxtla Gutiérrez, this being a matter within his competence.

Victorico Hernández Martínez and Agustín de la Torre Hernández

According to Amnesty International:

These two political leaders from Venustiano Carranza, both members of the "Emiliano Zapata" Peasant Organization, have been adopted as prisoners of conscience. Victorico Hernández Martínez, a leader of the "Casa del Pueblo", was arrested on 6 April 1981 on a charge of participating in the murder of José Fonseca Hernández, a peasant who was killed on 26 June 1980, allegedly by members of the "Casa del Pueblo". Also arrested, on the same charges, were Arturo Albores Velasco, a 31-year-old architecture student from the National Autonomous University of Mexico (UNAM), who was later released, and Agustín de la Torre Hernández, whose arrest took place on 24 February 1982. The three denied the charges and maintained that they had been arrested because of official opposition to their political activities.

Agustín de la Torre and Arturo Albores stated that while in custody they were kept incommunicado, subjected to torture and beaten and Arturo Albores claimed that this had caused him to suffer a perforated eardrum. The prisoners' request for release on grounds of insufficient evidence was turned down by the judge and their appeal was dismissed. However, the Attorney General of the state dropped the legal proceedings against Arturo Albores Velasco, who was freed on 4 December 1982.

On 4 November 1983, Victorico Hernández Martínez and Agustín de la Torre Hernández were found guilty of murder and sentenced to 12 years' imprisonment. In the case of the former, the sentence was passed two years after his arrest. Amnesty International also states that both prisoners submitted an *amparo* appeal to the Supreme Court of the Nation against this sentence and at the time of preparing its memorandum the ruling to reduce or annul the sentences was still awaited. It further points out that both individuals have played a leading role in their organization and community in efforts to recover communal lands, which has aroused the opposition of landowners, and that neither of them appears to have been involved in past acts of violence or to have advocated its use to achieve their aims.

Our inquiries show that:

Victorico Hernández Martínez and Agustín de la Torre Vázquez were sentenced to 12 years' imprisonment for their part in the simple murder with intent of José Fonseca Alvarez, in a judgment handed down by the judge of first instance of the judicial district of La Libertad. An appeal was lodged against the sentence and the criminal branch of the High Court of Justice of the state of Chiapas decided, in appeal No.982/83, to uphold the sentence imposed in the earlier proceedings. The sentenced people submitted an *amparo* appeal, which was directly registered as No.4380/84 in the Supreme Court of Justice of the Nation. It is recorded in the file that on 26 June 1980, José Antonio Espinoza Villa Toro, the person who found the body, reported the death of José Fonseca Hernández to the Agent of the Public Ministry in the town of Venustiano Carranza. The official inspection of Fonseca Hernández' lifeless body revealed four lacerations caused by a machete, the first one affecting bones and encephalic matter, another causing a fracture at the base of the skull, another in the cervical region and the fourth affecting skin and bone tissue; also visible were three bullet-holes produced by a .22 calibre weapon, in the right pectoral region, the upper thigh and the gluteal region.

The witness José Mendoza Mendoza said that on the day of the incident he saw Fonseca Hernández running, followed by more than 40 community members from the "Casa del Pueblo", with Victorico Hernández Martínez at their head. He was carrying a pistol in his right hand, which he saw when Victorico Hernández Martínez fired two shots at Fonseca Hernández, who fell to the ground grasping his hip and legs. Victorico Hernández Martínez went up to within two metres of the deceased and fired a third shot, aiming at the chest. As he still did not die, but tried to raise himself from the ground, the community members José María Hernández Martínez, Agustín de la Torre Vázquez and Antonio González slashed him behind the head with their machetes.

The witnesses José Mendoza Martínez, José Coutiño and Pedro Calvo Hidalgo are generally in agreement with the above statement and only add that the group that was pursuing Fonseca Hernández was shouting: "Stop him, stop him, there he is!" and that Victorico Hernández Martínez was at the head of the crowd. Another witness, Mariano Ramírez Calvo, said that he saw Victorico Hernández Martínez, armed with a pistol, fire shots at the deceased and that Agustín de la Torre Vázquez, José María Hernández and Antonio Vázquez finished him off with their machetes.

In his defence, Victorico Hernández Martínez declared that on the day of the incident he was working on a plot of land belonging to Roldán López García. This testimony and others were dismissed by the court on the grounds that they were submitted long after the events took place.

Consequently, in point four in the chapter of *considerandos* (whereas clauses) in the register of *amparo* appeals, the infringements cited by Victorico Hernández Martínez and Agustín de la Torre Hernández were shown to be unfounded. It was noted that the appeal court made a careful assessment of the available evidence and was thus correct in confirming the fact of the murder of José Fonseca Hernández and the guilt of the appellants, and in upholding the verdict and the sentence of 12 years' imprisonment, imposed with equality on the individuals concerned; also in its denial of *amparo* and the protection of federal justice. The decision was taken unanimously, on 19 August 1985, in the first courtroom of the Supreme Court of Justice of the Nation, made up of Fernando Castellanos Tena (President), Francisco H. Pavon Vasconcelos, Raúl Cuevas Mantecón, Santiago Rodríguez Roldán and Luis Fernández Doblado (court reporter).

Regarding the cases mentioned in Table 2, "Killings reported in the districts of Venustiano Carranza and Villa de las Rosas between 1965 and 1985", the following information has been obtained:

Victim	Date	Remarks
José Cordoba Ayar	1966	Penal action recommended.
Manuel Gómez Ortega	1970	The trial was in accordance with legal requirements.
Bartolomé Martínez Villatorio Guadalupe Vázquez Gómez	1975	No progress. The culprits have not been identified.
Miguel de la Cruz	1979	The government has no record of any report, nor has any investigation been initiated in Villa de las Rosas or Venustiano Carranza (as with the case of Elpidio Vázquez Vázquez, in which the authorities were excluded).
Alfredo Morales Molina	1980	Preliminary investigation 24/980 was put in hand and legal proceedings were continued but nobody came forward to testify against the accused, and the case

122

Cándido Velázquez Ruiz

inquiry was therefore shelved.
(The case is similar to that of
Elpidio Vázquez Vázquez.)
1982 Preliminary investigation 226/982
into this murder was opened and
testimonial evidence indicated
that Angel Flores, "El Zope",
was the culprit. An arrest order
was issued but has not yet been
carried out.

With regard to the information received direct from the state Attorney
General's office, the situation is as follows:

Accused	Remarks
Teodoro Vázquez Arias*	Now in detention in the Islas Marías (penal colony).
Peasants in the *ejidos* of "La Pimienta" and "Hotochen"	No progress. (There has been no cooperation from the peasants.)
Q.R.R. (Preliminary* Investigation 101/983)	No progress. (No cooperation.)
Members of the State Public Security Police*	No progress.
Serlin Morales and others*	No progress (the offences yet have to be certified).

*Note: these cases are not referred to in Amnesty International's
memorandum.

Annexes

Tzaclum (Tzacacum) Chalchihuitán

Annex 1

Forty village representatives, who, among others, were present at the town council meetings in Chalchihuitán on 13 and 23 March 1983 and who participated in the events:

1. NICOLAS LOPEZ GOMEZ
2. AGUSTIN RODRIGUEZ PEREZ
3. SALVADOR LOPEZ NUÑEZ   (leader — detained)
4. NICOLAS SANCHEZ PEREZ
5. DOMINGO PEREZ GOMEZ
6. MARTIN LUNA VAZQUEZ
7. DOMINGO SANCHEZ PEREZ   (leader)
8. CANDIDO DIAZ PEREZ   (detained)
9. MANUEL RODRIGUEZ SANCHEZ   (detained)
10. AGUSTIN RODRIGUEZ DOMINGUEZ   (detained)
11. NICOLAS PEREZ GOMEZ   (detained)
12. MANUEL AGUILAR PEREZ
13. PEDRO GOMEZ NUÑEZ
14. MARTIN PEREZ LOPEZ
15. AGUSTIN LOPEZ GOMEZ
16. CRISTOBAL PEREZ GIRON
17. MARTIN PEREZ DIAZ   (detained)
18. MANUEL GOMEZ GIRON
19. MELCHOR DIAZ GOMEZ
20. ENRIQUE LOPEZ GOMEZ   (detained)
21. SALVADOR LOPEZ NUÑEZ
22. DOMINGO GOMEZ LOPEZ
23. NICOLAS GOMEZ GIRON   (detained)
24. PEDRO NUÑEZ LOPEZ
25. MARIANO DIAZ GIRON   (detained)
26. ENRIQUE GOMEZ LOPEZ
27. PEDRO GOMEZ LOPEZ
28. MARIANO LOPEZ GIRON
29. NICOLAS LOPEZ GIRON
30. MARIANO GOMEZ GIRON
31. MARIANO GARCIA GOMEZ
32. DOMINGO DIAZ GIRON

124

33. LORENZO GIRON PEREZ
34. AGUSTIN GOMEZ LOPEZ
35. NICOLAS SANCHEZ PEREZ
36. SALVADOR GIRON DIAZ   (religious leader, assailant,
                                 municipal president, leader)
37. NICOLAS LOPEZ GOMEZ   (detained)
38. NICOLAS SANCHEZ PEREZ
39. SALVADOR GIRON DIAZ   (leader)
40. NICOLAS LOPEZ GOMEZ

Annex 2
List of those killed in Tzaclum (Tzacacum), municipality of
Chalchihuitán:
1. NAZARIA DIAZ LOPEZ
2. MANUEL LOPEZ DIAZ
3. MARIO PEREZ LOPEZ
4. MARIA LOPEZ PEREZ   (minor)
5. MANUEL LOPEZ GIRON
6. MARTIN LOPEZ DIAZ
7. DOMINGO NUÑEZ LOPEZ
8. BARTOLO NUÑEZ DIAZ
9. AGUSTIN PEREZ DIAZ
10. SEBASTIAN NUÑEZ LOPEZ
11. MARIANO NUÑEZ LOPEZ

Annex 3
Religious leaders and assailants:
1. SALVADOR GIRON DIAZ   (Paraje Pom)
2. NICOLAS LOPEZ GOMEZ   (Paraje Zinzón) (sentenced)
3. NICOLAS PEREZ GIRON   (Paraje Balo)
4. PEDRO GIRON LOPEZ   (Paraje Tzaclum)
5. MARTIN NUÑEZ DIAZ
6. DOMINGO SANCHEZ PEREZ
7. NICOLAS SANCHEZ PEREZ
8. SALVADOR LOPEZ NUÑEZ   (sentenced)

Annex 4
Detainees placed at the disposal of the state Attorney General:
1. NICOLAS LOPEZ GOMEZ   (religious leader from Paraje
                                 Zinzon)
2. DOMINGO GOMEZ LOPEZ
3. SALVADOR LOPEZ NUÑEZ   (leader)
4. MARIANO GARCIA PEREZ
5. NICOLAS PEREZ GOMEZ
6. NICOLAS GOMEZ GIRON
7. AGUSTIN RODRIGUEZ DOMINGUEZ
8. MARTIN PEREZ DIAZ
9. LORENZO GIRON PEREZ

10. MANUEL RODRIGUEZ SANCHEZ
11. CANDIDO DIAZ PEREZ
12. MARIANO DIAZ GIRON
13. ENRIQUE LOPEZ GOMEZ
14. VICENTE GARCIA GOMEZ
15. MARIANO GOMEZ GOMEZ
16. MARTIN GARCIA GIRON
17. CRISTOBAL PEREZ GIRON
18. MANUEL GOMEZ GIRON
19. MARTIN PEREZ DIAZ or DIAZ PEREZ
20. MANUEL DIAZ GOMEZ

Annex 5
Individuals against whom arrest warrants were issued for the crimes of criminal conspiracy, wounding, first degree murder and causing damage to property:

1. SALVADOR GIRON DIAZ	(main ringleader, religious leader and municipal president of Chalchihuitán)
2. NICOLAS PEREZ GIRON	(religious leader of the Paraje Balo)
3. PEDRO GIRON LOPEZ	(religious leader of the Paraje Tzaclum)
4. MARTIN NUÑEZ DIAZ	(religious leader and assailant)
5. MARTIN PEREZ NUÑEZ	
6. MARTIN GARCIA NUÑEZ	
7. CRISTOBAL PEREZ DIAZ	
8. DOMINGO DIAZ GIRON	(village representative, present at the meetings on 13 and 23 March 1983)
9. NICOLAS GOMEZ LOPEZ	
10. MARIANO GARCIA GOMEZ	(village representative, present at the meetings on 13 and 23 March 1983)
11. NICOLAS LOPEZ GIRON	
12. ENRIQUE GOMEZ LOPEZ	(village representative, present at the meetings on 13 and 23 March 1983)
13. PEDRO GOMEZ LOPEZ	(village representative, present at the meetings on 13 and 23 March 1983)
14. PEDRO NUÑEZ LOPEZ	(village representative, present at the meetings on 13 and 23 March 1983)
15. MARIANO DIAZ GIRON	(village representative, present at the meetings on 13 and 23 March 1983)

16. MANUEL GOMEZ GIRON	(village representative, present at the meetings on 13 and 23 March 1983)
17. MELCHOR DIAZ GOMEZ	(village representative, present at the meetings on 13 and 23 March 1983)
18. MARTIN LUNA VAZQUEZ	(village representative, present at the meetings on 13 and 23 March 1983)
19. MANUEL AGUILAR PEREZ	(village representative, present at the meetings on 13 and 23 March 1983)
20. DOMINGO SANCHEZ PEREZ	(village representative, present at the meetings on 13 and 23 March 1983, ring-leader)
21. NICOLAS SANCHEZ PEREZ	(village representative, present at the meetings on 13 and 23 March 1983, ring-leader)
22. DOMINGO PEREZ GOMEZ	(village representative, present at the meetings on 13 and 23 March 1983)
23. SALVADOR LOPEZ NUÑEZ	(village representative, present at the meetings on 13 and 23 March 1983)
24. DOMINGO DIAZ GIRON	(village representative, present at the meetings on 13 and 23 March 1983)
25. MARTIN GOMEZ DIAZ	

Annex 6

Sentenced to 21 years' imprisonment for the crimes of wounding, murder and damage to property:

1. NICOLAS LOPEZ GOMEZ	(religious leader from the Paraje Zinzon, assailant, he retracted his declarations)
2. MARIANO GOMEZ GOMEZ	(placed at the disposal of the authorities on 13 April 1983, he retracted his declarations)
3. MARIANO GARCIA PEREZ.	(placed at the disposal of the authorities on 13 April 1983, he retracted his declarations)
4. MARTIN GARCIA GIRON	(placed at the disposal of the authorities on 13 April 1983, he retracted his declarations)
5. VICENTE GARCIA GOMEZ	(placed at the disposal of the authorities on 13 April 1983, he retracted his declarations)

6. MARIANO GOMEZ GIRON (village representative, he retracted his declarations)

7. NICOLAS GOMEZ GIRON (placed at the disposal of the authorities on 13 April 1983, village representative, he retracted his declarations)

8. CANDIDO DIAZ PEREZ (placed at the disposal of the authorities on 13 April 1983, village representative, he retracted his declarations)

9. MANUEL RODRIGUEZ SANCHEZ (placed at the disposal of the authorities on 13 April 1983, village representative)

10. MARTIN PEREZ DIAZ (placed at the disposal of the authorities on 13 April 1983, village representative, he retracted his declarations)

11. DOMINGO GOMEZ LOPEZ (placed at the disposal of the authorities on 13 April 1983, village representative, he retracted his declarations)

12. NICOLAS PEREZ GOMEZ (placed at the disposal of the authorities on 13 April 1983, village representative, he retracted his declarations)

13. LORENZO GIRON PEREZ (placed at the disposal of the authorities on 13 April 1983, village representative, he retracted his declarations)

14. SALVADOR LOPEZ NUÑEZ (placed at the disposal of the authorities on 13 April 1983, village representative, he retracted his declarations)

15. AGUSTIN RODRIGUEZ DOMINGUEZ (placed at the disposal of the authorities on 13 April 1983, village representative, he retracted his declarations)

16. ENRIQUE LOPEZ GOMEZ (placed at the disposal of the authorities on 13 April 1983, village representative, he retracted his declarations)

17. MANUEL DIAZ GOMEZ (placed at the disposal of the Public Ministry)

18. MANUEL GOMEZ GIRON (placed at the disposal of the Public Ministry, village representative)

19. NICOLAS GOMEZ LOPEZ

20. CRISTOBAL PEREZ GIRON (placed at the disposal of the
Public Ministry, village
representative)
21. AGUSTIN GOMEZ LOPEZ (village representative)

The case of Domingo Calvo Espinoza and eight others

Annex 7
List of those killed from "La Casa del Pueblo":
1. JOSE MENDOZA MORALES
2. BARTOLOME RAMIREZ GOMEZ
3. DOMINGO CALVO ESPINOZA
4. JOSE ESPINOZA DE LA TORRE
5. CARALAMPIO GOMEZ MARTINEZ
6. PEDRO GOMEZ HERNANDEZ
7. AUGUSTO HERNANDEZ PEREZ
8. SEGUNDO ADOLFO REYES HERNANDEZ
9. JOSE JIMENEZ DE LA TORRE

Wounded:
1. BARTOLO HERNANDEZ GOMEZ
2. JULIO LOPEZ VELASCO
3. JOSE GOMEZ MARTINEZ
4. SEBASTIAN RAMIREZ HIDALGO

Annex 8
Result of paraffin wax test (Harrison):
Negative
1. AUGUSTO HERNANDEZ PEREZ (killed)
2. DOMINGO CALVO ESPINOZA (killed)
3. JULIO LOPEZ VAZQUEZ (wounded)
4. SEBASTIAN RAMIREZ HIDALGO (wounded)
5. JOSE GOMEZ MARTINEZ (wounded)
6. ARTURO HERNANDEZ GOMEZ

Positive
1. JOSE MENDOZA MORALES (killed)
2. JOSE JIMENEZ DE LA TORRE (killed)
3. PEDRO GOMEZ HERNANDEZ (killed)
4. CARALAMPIO GOMEZ MARTINEZ (killed)

Annex 9
Acquitted by the court of first instance:
1. BARTOLOME JIMENEZ DE LA TORRE
2. RUFINO MENDEZ ALCAZAR

3. JOSE GOMEZ SOLANO
4. FERNANDO VIVES ROBLES
5. MIGUEL MENDOZA ESPINOZA
6. MANUEL GOMEZ MENDOZA
7. SEBASTIAN ESPINOZA MARTINEZ
8. BARTOLOME ESPINOZA MENDOZA
9. JUAN VAZQUEZ VELASCO
10. JOSE CALVO VAZQUEZ
11. BARTOLOME GOMEZ ESPINOZA

Appendix II

Amnesty International 12-Point Program for the Prevention of Torture

Torture is a fundamental violation of human rights, condemned by the General Assembly of the United Nations as an offence to human dignity and prohibited under national and international law. Yet torture persists, daily and across the globe. In Amnesty International's experience, legislative prohibition is not enough. Immediate steps are needed to confront torture and other cruel, inhuman or degrading treatment or punishment wherever they occur and to eradicate them totally.

Amnesty International calls on all governments to implement the following 12-Point Program for the Prevention of Torture. It invites concerned individuals and organizations to join in promoting the program. Amnesty International believes that the implementation of these measures is a positive indication of a government's commitment to abolish torture and to work for its abolition worldwide.

1. Official condemnation of torture
The highest authorities of every country should demonstrate their total opposition to torture. They should make clear to all law-enforcement personnel that torture will not be tolerated under any circumstances.

2. Limits on incommunicado detention
Torture often takes place while the victims are held incommunicado — unable to contact people outside who could help them or find out what is happening to them. Governments should adopt safeguards to ensure that incommunicado detention does not become an opportunity for torture. It is vital that all prisoners be brought before a judicial authority promptly after being taken into custody and that relatives, lawyers and doctors have prompt and regular access to them.

3. No secret detention
In some countries torture takes place in secret centres, often after the victims are made to "disappear". Governments should ensure that prisoners are held in publicly recognized places, and that accurate information about their whereabouts is made available to relatives and lawyers.

4. Safeguards during interrogation and custody
Governments should keep procedures for detention and interrogation under regular review. All prisoners should be promptly told of their rights, including the right to lodge complaints about their treatment. There should be regular independent visits of inspection to places of detention. An important safeguard against torture would be the separation of authorities responsible for detention from those in charge of interrogation.

5. Independent investigation of reports of torture
Governments should ensure that all complaints and reports of torture are impartially and effectively investigated. The methods and findings of such investigations should be made public. Complainants and witnesses should be protected from intimidation.

6. No use of statements extracted under torture
Governments should ensure that confessions or other evidence obtained through torture may never be invoked in legal proceedings.

7. Prohibition of torture in law
Governments should ensure that acts of torture are punishable offences under the criminal law. In accordance with international law, the prohibition of torture must not be suspended under any circumstances, including states of war or other public emergency.

8. Prosecution of alleged torturers
Those responsible for torture should be brought to justice. This principle should apply wherever they happen to be, wherever the crime was committed and whatever the nationality of the perpetrators or victims. There should be no "safe haven" for torturers.

9. Training procedures
It should be made clear during the training of all officials involved in the custody, interrogation or treatment of prisoners that torture is a criminal act. They should be instructed that they are obliged to refuse to obey any order to torture.

10. Compensation and rehabilitation
Victims of torture and their dependants should be entitled to obtain financial compensation. Victims should be provided with appropriate medical care or rehabilitation.

11. International response
Governments should use all available channels to intercede with governments accused of torture. Inter-governmental mechanisms should be established and used to investigate reports of torture urgently and to take effective action against it. Governments should ensure that military, security or police transfers or training do not facilitate the practice of torture.

12. Ratification of international instruments
All governments should ratify international instruments containing safeguards and remedies against torture, including the International Covenant on Civil and Political Rights and its Optional Protocol which provides for individual complaints.

The 12-Point Program was adopted by Amnesty International in October 1983 as part of the organization's Campaign for the Abolition of Torture.

Amnesty International —
a worldwide campaign

In recent years, people throughout the world have become more and more aware of the urgent need to protect human rights effectively in every part of the world.

• Countless men and women are in prison for their beliefs. They are being held as prisoners of conscience in scores of countries—in crowded jails, in labour camps and in remote prisons.

• Thousands of political prisoners are being held under administrative detention orders and denied any possibility of a trial or an appeal.

• Others are forcibly confined in psychiatric hospitals or secret detention camps.

• Many are forced to endure relentless, systematic torture.

• More than a hundred countries retain the death penalty.

• Political leaders and ordinary citizens are becoming the victims of abductions, "disappearances" and killings, carried out both by government forces and opposition groups.

An international effort

To end secret arrests, torture and killing requires organized and worldwide effort. Amnesty International is part of that effort.

Launched as an independent organization over 20 years ago, Amnesty International is open to anyone prepared to work universally for the release of prisoners of conscience, for fair trials for political prisoners and for an end to torture and executions.

The movement now has members and supporters in more than 160 countries. It is independent of any government, political group, ideology, economic interest or religious creed.

The mandate

Amnesty International is playing a specific role in the international protection of human rights.

It seeks the *release* of men and women detained anywhere because of their beliefs, colour, sex, ethnic origin, language or religious creed, provided they have not used or advocated violence. These are termed *prisoners of conscience.*

It works for *fair and prompt trials* for *all political prisoners* and works on behalf of such people detained without charge or trial.

It opposes the *death penalty* and *torture* or other cruel, inhuman or degrading treatment or punishment of *all prisoners* without reservation.

Amnesty International acts on the basis of the Universal Declaration of Human Rights and other international convenants. Amnesty International is convinced of the indivisibility and mutual dependence of all human rights. Through the practical work for prisoners within its mandate, Amnesty International participates in the wider promotion and protection of human rights in the civil, political, economic, social and cultural spheres.

Amnesty International does not oppose or support any government or political system. Its members around the world include supporters of differing systems who agree on the defence of all people in all countries against imprisonment for their beliefs, and against torture and execution.

Amnesty International at work

The working methods of Amnesty International are based on the principle of international responsibility for the protection of human rights. The movement tries to take action wherever and whenever there are violations of those human rights falling within its mandate. Since it was founded, Amnesty International groups have intervened on behalf of more than 25,000 prisoners in over a hundred countries with widely differing ideologies.

A unique aspect of the work of Amnesty International groups—placing the emphasis on the need for *international* human rights work—is the fact that each group works on behalf of prisoners held in countries other than its own. At least two prisoner cases are assigned to each group; the cases are balanced geographically and politically to ensure impartiality.

There are now 3,341 local Amnesty International groups throughout the world. There are sections in 43 countries (in Africa, Asia, the Americas, Europe and the Middle East) and individual members, subscribers and supporters in more than 120 other countries. Members do not work on cases in their own countries. No section, group or member is expected to provide information on their own country and no section, group or member has any responsibility for action taken or statements issued by the international organization concerning their own country.

Continuous research

The movement attaches the highest importance to balanced and accurate reporting of facts. All its activities depend on meticulous research into allegations of human rights violations. The International Secretariat in London (with a staff of 175, comprising 30 nationalities) has a Research Department which collects and analyses information from a wide variety of sources. These include hundreds of newspapers and journals, government bulletins, transcriptions of radio broadcasts, reports from lawyers and humanitarian organizations, as well as letters from prisoners and their families. Amnesty International also sends fact-finding missions for on-the-spot investigations and to observe trials, meet prisoners and interview government officials. Amnesty International takes full responsibility for its published reports and if proved wrong on any point is prepared to issue a correction.

Once the relevant facts are established, information is sent to sections and groups for action. The members then start the work of trying to protect the individuals whose human rights are reported to have been violated. They send letters to government ministers and embassies. They organize public meetings, arrange special publicity events, such as vigils at appropriate government offices or embassies, and try to interest newspapers in the cases they have taken up. They ask their friends and colleagues to help in the effort. They collect signatures for international petitions and raise money to send relief, such as medicine, food and clothing, to the prisoners and their families.

A permanent campaign

In addition to case work on behalf of individual prisoners, Amnesty International members campaign for the abolition of torture and the death penalty. This includes trying to prevent torture and executions when people have been taken to known torture centres or sentenced to death. Volunteers in dozens of countries can be alerted in such cases, and within hours hundreds of telegrams and other appeals can be on their way to the government, prison or detention centre.

Symbol of
Amnesty International

Amnesty International condemns as a matter of principle the torture and execution of prisoners by *anyone*, including opposition groups. Governments have the responsibility of dealing with such abuses, acting in conformity with international standards for the protection of human rights.

In its efforts to mobilize world public opinion, Amnesty International neither supports nor opposes economic or cultural boycotts. It *does* take a stand against the international transfer of military, police or security equipment and expertise likely to be used by recipient governments to detain prisoners of conscience and to inflict torture and carry out executions.

Amnesty International does not grade governments or countries according to their record on human rights. Not only does repression in various countries prevent the free flow of information about human rights abuses, but the techniques of repression and their impact vary widely. Instead of attempting comparisons, Amnesty International concentrates on trying to end the specific violations of human rights in each case.

Policy and funds

Amnesty International is a democratically run movement. Every two years major policy decisions are taken by an International Council comprising representatives from all the sections. They elect an International Executive Committee to carry out their decisions and supervise the day-to-day running of the International Secretariat.

The organization is financed by its members throughout the world, by individual subscriptions and donations. Members pay fees and conduct fund-raising campaigns—they organize concerts and art auctions and are often to be seen on fund-raising drives at street corners in their neighbourhoods.

Its rules about accepting donations are strict and ensure that any funds received by any part of the organization do not compromise it in any way, affect its integrity, make it dependent on any donor, or limit its freedom of activity.

The organization's accounts are audited annually and are published with its annual report.

Amnesty International has formal relations with the United Nations (ECOSOC), UNESCO, the Council of Europe, the Organization of African Unity and the Organization of American States.